Barbecue

Bath · New York · Singapore · Hong Kong · Cologne · Delhi · Melbourne

This edition published by Parragon in 2010

Parragon Publishing
Queen Street House
4 Queen Street
Bath BA1 1HE, UK

ISBN 978-1-4075-9468-2

Printed in China

Notes for the Reader
This book uses imperial, metric, and U.S. cup measurements. Follow the same units of measurement throughout; do not mix imperial and metric. All spoon measurements are level: teaspoons are assumed to be 5 ml, and tablespoons are assumed to be 15 ml. Unless otherwise stated, milk is assumed to be whole, eggs and individual vegetables, such as potatoes, are medium, and pepper is freshly ground black pepper.

The times given are an approximate guide only. Preparation times differ according to the techniques used by different people and the cooking times may also vary from those given as a result of the type of oven used. Optional ingredients, variations, or serving suggestions have not been included in the calculations.

Recipes using raw or very lightly cooked eggs should be avoided by infants, the elderly, pregnant women, convalescents, and anyone with a chronic condition. Pregnant and breast-feeding women are advised to avoid eating peanuts and peanut products. People with nut allergies should be aware that some of the prepared ingredients used in the recipes in this book may contain nuts. Always check the packaging before use.

Picture acknowledgments
The publisher would like to thank Getty Images for permission to reproduce copyright material for the front cover

Barbecue

introduction

Eating outdoors is always fun and there's something especially appetizing about food cooked on a barbecue. Everyone enjoys themselves—old and young, family and friends, even the cook—and there are great dishes to suit all tastes and budgets. In fact, the variety of barbecue dishes and the range of ingredients are surprising—from traditional burgers, steak, and ribs to fabulous whole fish, butterflied poultry, vegetable packages, and even fruity desserts. You can keep things really simple with cheeseburgers, salad greens, and prepared dressing or push the boat out with

a choice of marinated meats, chargrilled vegetables, rice salad, and homemade salsas, finishing triumphantly with fruit kabobs. One of the best things is that however much preparation you want to undertake, it's all done in advance.

Safety is important but it's mostly a matter of common sense. Follow the manufacturer's instructions for positioning, lighting, using, and cleaning your barbecue. If using charcoal, remember to light it well in advance and

have a bucket of water and/or sand nearby just in case. Make sure somebody is responsible for keeping an eye on any children and pets and never leave a lit barbecue unattended. Don't take raw food outdoors until you are ready to start cooking and keep it covered. Keep sauces and dressings cool, especially if, like mayonnaise, they contain raw eggs. Use separate tools for raw and cooked meat and check that poultry and pork in particular are thoroughly cooked.

Pierce the thickest part with the point of a sharp knife and, if there's any trace of pink or red in the juices, cook the meat for a little longer and check again. Drain off marinades before putting meat or fish on the grill to avoid flare-up, and if you're going to use a marinade as a sauce, make sure you bring it to a boil first.

best burgers

It's hard to imagine a barbecue without burgers and, once you've tasted the homemade variety, you'll always include them in future. Not only is the flavor so much better than store-bought burgers, but there are no additives and you know exactly what has gone into the mix, so you can easily control the size and the quantities of fat and salt. What's more, a barbecue is for grilling, not frying, so all of a sudden this demon junk food becomes a less-fatty, fully paid-up member of the healthy diet club.

The burger has come a long way from its humble beginnings among German immigrants to the United States and you will be amazed at the variety and range of recipes. You can use all kinds of meat, from traditional ground steak to duck, create tasty fish burgers, and make superb vegetarian versions from ingredients as different as beans and sweet potatoes. "Extras" now extend far beyond merely adding a slice of cheese—although a genuine homemade cheeseburger is a barbecue delight—and recipes include marinades, spices, herbs, vegetables, nuts, and fruit. There's sure to be the perfect burger for everyone, whether meaty and full of fiery Cajun flavors or a light-textured, moist mixture of apples and cheese—even for people who profess to dislike them.

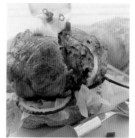

the classic hamburger

ingredients

SERVES 4–6

1 lb/450 g sirloin or top
   round, freshly ground

1 onion, grated

2–4 garlic cloves, crushed

2 tsp whole-grain mustard

2 tbsp olive oil

1 lb/450 g onions, finely
   sliced

2 tsp brown sugar

pepper

hamburger buns, to serve

method

1 Place the ground beef, onion, garlic, mustard, and pepper in a large bowl and mix together. Shape into 4–6 equal-size burgers, then cover and let chill for 30 minutes.

2 Meanwhile, heat the oil in a heavy-bottom skillet. Add the onions and sauté over low heat for 10–15 minutes, or until the onions have caramelized. Add the sugar after 8 minutes and stir occasionally during cooking. Drain well on paper towels and keep warm.

3 Preheat the barbecue. Cook the burgers over hot coals for 3–5 minutes on each side, or until cooked to personal preference. Serve in hamburger buns with the onions.

cheese & bacon burgers

ingredients

SERVES 4

1 lb/450 g best ground steak

4 onions

2–4 garlic cloves, crushed

2–3 tsp grated fresh
    horseradish or 1–1$\frac{1}{2}$ tbsp
    creamed horseradish

8 lean Canadian bacon slices

2 tbsp corn oil

4 cheese slices

pepper

hamburger buns, to serve

method

1 Place the ground steak in a large bowl. Finely grate 1 of the onions and add to the ground steak.

2 Add the garlic, horseradish, and pepper to the steak mixture in the bowl. Mix together, then shape into 4 equal-size burgers. Wrap each burger in 2 slices of bacon, then cover and let chill for 30 minutes.

3 Preheat the barbecue. Slice the remaining onions. Heat the oil in a skillet. Add the onions and cook over medium heat for 8–10 minutes, stirring frequently, until the onions are golden brown. Drain on paper towels and keep warm.

4 Cook the burgers over hot coals for 3–5 minutes on each side, or until cooked through. Top each burger with a slice of cheese for the last minute of cooking. Serve in hamburger buns.

hamburgers with chile & basil

ingredients

SERVES 4

1 lb 7 oz/650 g ground beef

1 red bell pepper, seeded and
    finely chopped

1 garlic clove, finely chopped

2 small red chiles, seeded
    and finely chopped

1 tbsp chopped fresh basil

$1/2$ tsp ground cumin

salt and pepper

sprigs of fresh basil,
    to garnish

hamburger buns, to serve

method

1 Put the ground beef, red bell pepper, garlic, chiles, chopped basil, and cumin into a bowl and mix until well combined. Season with salt and pepper. Using your hands, form the mixture into burger shapes.

2 Preheat the barbecue. Cook the burgers over hot coals for 5–8 minutes on each side, or until cooked through. Garnish with sprigs of basil and serve in hamburger buns.

blt burger with asparagus

ingredients

SERVES 4–6

8 oz/225 g Canadian bacon
   slices

1 lb/450 g best ground steak

1 onion, grated

2–4 garlic cloves, crushed

1–2 tbsp corn oil

salt and pepper

dip

6 oz/175 g baby asparagus
   spears

1 tbsp lemon juice

1 small ripe avocado, peeled,
   pitted, and finely chopped

2 firm tomatoes, peeled,
   seeded, and finely
   chopped

$2/3$ cup sour cream

salt and pepper

to serve

hamburger buns

lettuce leaves

tomato slices

method

1 Remove any rind and fat from the bacon slices and chop finely.

2 Place the bacon, ground steak, onion, and garlic in a large bowl and mix well. Shape into 4–6 equal-size burgers, then cover and let chill for 30 minutes.

3 Trim the asparagus and cook in a pan of lightly salted boiling water for 5 minutes, then drain and plunge into cold water. When cold, drain and finely chop half the spears into a bowl. Sprinkle the lemon juice over the avocado. Stir in the avocado, tomatoes, and sour cream. Add salt and pepper to taste, cover, and let chill until required.

4 Preheat the barbecue. Lightly brush the burgers with the remaining oil, and cook over hot coals for 5–6 minutes on each side, or until cooked to personal preference. Serve the burgers in hamburger buns with lettuce, topped with a tomato slice, asparagus spear, and a dollop of the dip.

minty lamb burgers

ingredients

SERVES 4–6

1 red bell pepper, seeded and
     cut into quarters
1 yellow bell pepper, seeded
     and cut into quarters
1 red onion, cut into thick
     wedges
1 baby eggplant (4 oz/115 g),
     cut into wedges
2 tbsp olive oil
1 lb/450 g fresh ground lamb
2 tbsp freshly grated
     Parmesan cheese
1 tbsp chopped fresh mint
salt and pepper

minty mustard mayonnaise

4 tbsp mayonnaise
1 tsp Dijon mustard
1 tbsp chopped fresh mint

to serve

hamburger buns
shredded lettuce
grilled vegetables, such as
     bell peppers and cherry
     tomatoes

method

1 Preheat the broiler to medium. Place the bell peppers, onion, and eggplant on a foil-lined broiler rack, brush the eggplant with 1 tablespoon of the oil, and cook under the hot broiler for 10–12 minutes, or until charred. Remove from the broiler, let cool, then peel the bell peppers. Place all the vegetables in a food processor and, using the pulse button, chop.

2 Add the ground lamb, Parmesan cheese, chopped mint, and salt and pepper to the food processor and blend until the mixture comes together. Scrape onto a board and shape into 4–6 equal-size burgers. Cover and let chill for at least 30 minutes.

3 To make the minty mustard mayonnaise, blend the mayonnaise with the mustard and chopped fresh mint. Cover and chill until required.

4 Preheat the barbecue. Lightly brush the burgers with the remaining oil, and cook over hot coals for 3–4 minutes on each side, or until cooked to personal preference. Serve the burgers in hamburger buns with the shredded lettuce and prepared mayonnaise, and a selection of grilled vegetables on the side.

lamb & feta cheese burgers

ingredients

SERVES 4–6

1 lb/450 g fresh ground lamb

8 oz/225 g feta cheese, crumbled

2 garlic cloves, crushed

6 scallions, finely chopped

$^1/_2$ cup prunes, chopped

2 tbsp pine nuts, toasted

1 cup fresh whole-wheat breadcrumbs

1 tbsp chopped fresh rosemary

1 tbsp corn oil

salt and pepper

method

1 Place the ground lamb in a large bowl with the feta, garlic, scallions, prunes, pine nuts, and breadcrumbs. Mix well, breaking up any lumps of meat.

2 Add the rosemary and salt and pepper to the lamb mixture in the bowl. Mix together, then shape into 4–6 equal-size burgers. Cover and let chill for 30 minutes.

3 Preheat the barbecue. Brush the burgers lightly with oil and cook over hot coals for 4 minutes before turning over and brushing with the remaining oil. Continue to cook for 4 minutes, or until cooked to personal preference. Serve.

pork burgers with tangy orange marinade

ingredients

SERVES 4–6

1 lb/450 g pork fillet, cut into
  small pieces

3 tbsp Seville orange
  marmalade

2 tbsp orange juice

1 tbsp balsamic vinegar

8 oz/225 g parsnips, cut into
  chunks

1 tbsp finely grated orange rind

2 garlic cloves, crushed

6 scallions, finely chopped

1 zucchini (6 oz/175 g), grated

1 tbsp corn oil

salt and pepper

lettuce leaves, to serve

hamburger buns, to serve

method

1 Place the pork in a shallow dish. Place the marmalade, orange juice, and vinegar in a small pan and heat, stirring, until the marmalade has melted. Pour the marinade over the pork. Cover and let stand for at least 30 minutes, or longer if time permits. Remove the pork, reserving the marinade. Grind the pork into a large bowl.

2 Meanwhile, cook the parsnips in a pan of boiling water for 15–20 minutes, or until cooked. Drain, then mash and add to the pork. Stir in the orange rind, garlic, scallions, zucchini, and salt and pepper to taste. Mix together, then shape into 4–6 equal-size burgers. Cover and let chill for at least 30 minutes.

3 Preheat the barbecue. When hot, lightly brush the burgers with oil and cook over hot coals for 4–6 minutes on each side, or until thoroughly cooked. Boil the reserved marinade for at least 5 minutes, then pour into a small pitcher or bowl. Serve with the lettuce leaves in hamburger buns.

barbecued cajun pork burgers

ingredients

SERVES 4–6

8 oz/225 g sweet potatoes,
    cut into chunks

1 lb/450 g fresh ground pork

1 apple, peeled, cored
    and grated

2 tsp Cajun seasoning

1 lb/450 g onions

1 tbsp chopped fresh cilantro

2 tbsp corn oil

8–12 lean Canadian bacon
    slices

salt and pepper

method

1 Cook the sweet potato in a pan of lightly salted boiling water for 15–20 minutes, or until soft when pierced with a fork. Drain well, then mash and set aside.

2 Place the ground pork in a bowl, add the mashed potato, grated apple, and Cajun seasoning. Grate 1 of the onions and add to the pork mixture with salt and pepper to taste and the chopped cilantro. Mix together, then shape into 4–6 equal-size burgers. Cover and let chill for 1 hour.

3 Slice the remaining onions. Heat 1 tablespoon of the oil in a skillet. Add the onions and cook over low heat for 10–12 minutes, stirring until soft. Remove the skillet from the heat and set aside. Wrap each burger in 2 slices of bacon.

4 Preheat the barbecue. Lightly brush the burgers with oil, and cook over hot coals for 5–6 minutes on each side, or until cooked to personal preference. Serve with the fried onions.

the ultimate chicken burger

ingredients

SERVES 4

4 large chicken breast fillets,
  skinned

1 large egg white

1 tbsp cornstarch

1 tbsp all-purpose flour

1 egg, beaten

1 cup fresh white
  breadcrumbs

2 beefsteak tomatoes, sliced

to serve

hamburger buns

shredded lettuce

mayonnaise

method

1 Place the chicken breasts between 2 sheets of nonstick parchment paper and flatten slightly using a meat mallet or a rolling pin. Beat the egg white and cornstarch together, then brush over the chicken. Cover and let chill for 30 minutes, then coat in the flour.

2 Place the egg and breadcrumbs in 2 separate bowls and coat the burgers first in the egg, allowing any excess to drip back into the bowl, then in the breadcrumbs.

3 Preheat the barbecue. When hot, add the burgers and cook over hot coals for 6–8 minutes on each side, or until thoroughly cooked. If you are in doubt, it is worth cutting one of the burgers in half. If there is any sign of pinkness, cook for a little longer. Add the tomato slices for the last 1–2 minutes of the cooking time to heat through. Serve the burgers in hamburger buns with the shredded lettuce, cooked tomato slices, and mayonnaise.

bacon-wrapped chicken burgers

ingredients

SERVES 4

1 lb/450 g fresh ground
   chicken
1 onion, grated
2 garlic cloves, crushed
$^1/_3$ cup pine nuts, toasted
$^1/_2$ cup grated Gruyère cheese
2 tbsp fresh snipped chives
2 tbsp whole-wheat flour
8 lean Canadian bacon slices
1–2 tbsp corn oil
salt and pepper

to serve

hamburger buns
shredded lettuce
red onion slices

method

1 Place the ground chicken, onion, garlic, pine nuts, cheese, chives, and salt and pepper to taste in a food processor. Using the pulse button, blend the mixture together using short bursts. Scrape out onto a board and shape into 4 equal-size burgers. Coat in the flour, then cover and let chill for 1 hour.

2 Wrap each burger with 2 bacon slices, securing in place with a wooden toothpick.

3 Preheat the barbecue. When hot, lightly brush the burgers with oil and cook over hot coals for 5–6 minutes on each side, or until thoroughly cooked through. Serve in hamburger buns with shredded lettuce and sliced red onion.

turkey & tarragon burgers

ingredients

SERVES 4

generous $\frac{1}{3}$ cup bulgur
    wheat
1 lb/450 g fresh ground
    turkey
1 tbsp finely grated orange
    rind
1 red onion, finely chopped
1 yellow bell pepper, seeded,
    peeled, and finely
    chopped
$\frac{1}{4}$ cup toasted slivered
    almonds
1 tbsp chopped fresh
    tarragon
1–2 tbsp corn oil
salt and pepper

to serve

jacket potatoes
tomato relish
lettuce leaves
tomato slices
onion slices

method

1 Cook the bulgur wheat in a pan of lightly salted boiling water for 10–15 minutes, or according to the package instructions.

2 Drain the bulgur wheat and place in a bowl with the ground turkey, orange rind, onion, yellow bell pepper, almonds, tarragon, and salt and pepper. Mix together, then shape into 4 equal-size burgers. Cover and let chill for 1 hour.

3 Preheat the barbecue. When hot, lightly brush the burgers with oil and cook over hot coals for 5–6 minutes on each side, or until thoroughly cooked through. Serve the burgers with jacket potatoes, tomato relish, lettuce and sliced tomato and onion.

mexican turkey burgers

ingredients

SERVES 4

1 lb/450 g fresh ground turkey

7 oz/200 g canned refried
  beans

2–4 garlic cloves, crushed

1–2 fresh jalapeño chiles,
  seeded and finely chopped

2 tbsp tomato paste

1 tbsp chopped fresh cilantro

1 tbsp corn oil

salt and pepper

to serve

hamburger buns

shredded lettuce

salsa

guacamole

tortilla chips

method

1 Place the ground turkey in a bowl and break up any large lumps. Beat the refried beans until smooth, then add to the turkey.

2 Add the garlic, chiles, tomato paste, cilantro, salt, and pepper and mix together. Shape into 4 equal-size burgers, then cover and let chill for 1 hour.

3 Preheat the barbecue. When hot, lightly brush the burgers with oil and cook over hot coals for 5–6 minutes on each side, or until thoroughly cooked through. Serve the Mexican turkey burgers in hamburger buns with shredded lettuce, salsa, and guacamole, with tortilla chips on the side.

duck burgers with sweet apple & plum relish

ingredients

SERVES 4

2 apples

1 lb/450 g fresh duck breast meat, fat removed and ground

3 tbsp prepared Thai plum sauce

6 scallions, finely chopped

2 garlic cloves, crushed

$1/3$ cup dried crushed chiles

scant $3/8$ cup dried cranberries

1 tbsp corn oil

1 tbsp butter

2–3 tsp raw brown sugar

sweet apple and plum relish

salt and pepper

mashed potatoes with red and green chiles, to serve

method

1 Peel, core, and grate 1 of the apples and place in a large bowl with the ground duck, 1 tablespoon of the plum sauce, scallions, garlic, $1/2$–1 teaspoon of chiles, half the cranberries, and salt and pepper to taste. Mix together, then shape into 4 equal-size burgers. Cover and let chill for 1 hour.

2 Preheat the barbecue. When hot, lightly brush the burgers with oil and cook over hot coals for 3–4 minutes on each side, or until cooked to personal preference. Keep warm.

3 Peel, core, and slice the remaining apple. Melt the butter in a skillet. Add the apple, sprinkle with the sugar, and cook for 3–4 minutes, or until slightly softened and lightly caramelized. Remove the skillet from the heat.

4 To make the relish, add the remaining chiles, cranberries, and plum sauce to the apple sauce and cook for 3 minutes, stirring occasionally. Serve the duck burgers on top of mashed potatoes with red and green chiles and pour the sweet apple and plum relish over the top.

fish burgers

ingredients

SERVES 4

5 oz/140 g potatoes, cut into
   chunks

8 oz/225 g cod fillet, skinned

8 oz/225 g haddock, skinned

1 tbsp grated lemon rind

1 tbsp chopped fresh parsley

1–2 tbsp all-purpose flour

1 egg, beaten

1^1/$_2$ cups fresh white
   breadcrumbs

2 tbsp corn oil

salt and pepper

hamburger buns, to serve

method

1 Cook the potatoes in a pan of lightly salted boiling water for 15–20 minutes, or until tender. Drain well and mash. Chop the fish into small pieces, then place in a food processor with the mashed potatoes, lemon rind, parsley, and salt and pepper to taste. Using the pulse button, blend together. Shape into 4 equal-size burgers and coat in the flour. Cover and let chill for 30 minutes.

2 Place the egg and breadcrumbs in 2 separate bowls and coat the burgers first in the egg, allowing any excess to drip back into the bowl, then in the breadcrumbs. Let chill for an additional 30 minutes.

3 Preheat the barbecue. Brush the burgers lightly with oil and cook over hot coals for 4–5 minutes on each side, or until golden and cooked through. Serve in toasted hamburger buns.

salmon burgers with spinach & pine nuts

ingredients

SERVES 4

$10^1/_2$ oz/300 g potatoes,
    cut into chunks

1 lb/450 g fresh salmon fillet,
    skinned

$3^3/_4$ cups fresh spinach leaves

$1/_3$ cup pine nuts, toasted

2 tbsp finely grated lemon
    rind

1 tbsp chopped fresh parsley

2 tbsp whole-wheat flour

scant 1 cup sour cream

$1^1/_2$-inch/4-cm piece
    cucumber, peeled and
    finely chopped

2 tbsp corn oil

salt and pepper

to serve

hamburger buns

mayonnaise

cherry tomatoes

method

1 Cook the potatoes in a pan of lightly salted boiling water for 15–20 minutes, or until tender. Drain well, then mash and set aside. Chop the salmon into chunks.

2 Reserve a few spinach leaves for serving, then blanch the remainder in a pan of boiling water for 2 minutes. Drain, squeezing out any excess moisture, then chop.

3 Place the spinach in a food processor with the salmon, potatoes, pine nuts, 1 tablespoon of the lemon rind, parsley, and salt and pepper and, using the pulse button, blend together. Shape into 4–6 equal-size burgers, then cover and let chill for 1 hour. Coat the burgers in the flour.

4 Mix the sour cream, remaining lemon rind, and cucumber together in a bowl, then cover and let chill until required.

5 Preheat the barbecue. When hot, lightly brush the burgers with oil and cook over hot coals for 4–6 minutes on each side, or until cooked through. Serve the burgers in hamburger buns with the reserved spinach leaves, with mayonnaise, and tomatoes on the side.

fresh tuna burgers with mango salsa

ingredients

SERVES 4–6

8 oz/225 g sweet potatoes, chopped

1 lb/450 g fresh tuna steaks

6 scallions, finely chopped

6 oz/175 g zucchini, grated

1 fresh red jalapeño chile, seeded and finely chopped

2 tbsp prepared mango chutney

1 tbsp corn oil

salt

lettuce leaves, to serve

mango salsa

1 large ripe mango, peeled and seeded

2 ripe tomatoes, finely chopped

1 fresh red jalapeño chile, seeded and finely chopped

$1^1/_2$-inch/4-cm piece cucumber, finely diced

1 tbsp chopped fresh cilantro

1–2 tsp honey

method

1 Cook the sweet potatoes in a pan of lightly salted boiling water for 15–20 minutes, or until tender. Drain well, then mash and place in a food processor. Cut the tuna into chunks and add to the potatoes.

2 Add the scallions, zucchini, chile, and mango chutney to the food processor and, using the pulse button, blend together. Shape into 4–6 equal-size burgers, then cover and let chill for 1 hour.

3 Meanwhile, make the salsa. Slice the mango flesh, reserving 8–12 good slices for serving. Finely chop the remainder, then mix with the tomatoes, chile, cucumber, cilantro, and honey. Mix well, then spoon into a small bowl. Cover and let stand for 30 minutes to allow the flavors to develop.

4 Preheat the barbecue. Brush the burgers lightly with oil and cook over hot coals for 4–6 minutes on each side, or until piping hot. Serve with the mango salsa, garnished with lettuce leaves and the reserved slices of mango.

the ultimate vegetarian burger

ingredients

SERVES 4–6

scant $1/2$ cup brown rice

14 oz/400 g canned
    flageolets, drained

scant 1 cup unsalted cashew
    nuts

3 garlic cloves

1 red onion, cut into wedges

$1/2$ cup corn kernels

2 tbsp tomato paste

1 tbsp chopped fresh oregano

2 tbsp whole-wheat flour

2 tbsp corn oil

salt and pepper

to serve

hamburger buns

lettuce leaves

tomato slices

cheese slices

method

1 Cook the rice in a pan of lightly salted boiling water for 20 minutes, or following the package instructions, until tender. Drain and place in a food processor.

2 Add the beans, nuts, garlic, onion, corn, tomato paste, oregano, and salt and pepper to the rice in the food processor and, using the pulse button, blend together. Shape into 4–6 equal-size burgers, then coat in the flour. Cover and let chill for 1 hour.

3 Preheat the barbecue. Brush the burgers lightly with oil and cook over hot coals for 5–6 minutes on each side, or until cooked and piping hot. Serve the burgers in hamburger buns with the lettuce leaves and tomato and cheese slices.

three-bean burgers with green mayo

ingredients

SERVES 4–6

10$^1/_2$ oz/300 g canned
cannellini beans, drained

10$^1/_2$ oz/300 g canned
black-eyed peas, drained

10$^1/_2$ oz/300 g canned red
kidney beans, drained and
rinsed

1 fresh red chile, deseeded

4 shallots, cut into quarters

2 celery stalks, coarsely
chopped

1 cup fresh whole-wheat
breadcrumbs

1 tbsp chopped fresh cilantro

2 tbsp whole-wheat flour

2 tbsp corn oil

salt and pepper

hamburger buns, to serve

green mayo

6 tbsp prepared mayonnaise

2 tbsp chopped fresh parsley
or mint

1 tbsp chopped cucumber

3 scallions, finely chopped

method

1 Place the beans, chile, shallots, celery, breadcrumbs, cilantro, and salt and pepper in a food processor and, using the pulse button, blend together. Shape into 4–6 equal-size burgers, then cover and let chill for 1 hour. Coat the burgers lightly in the flour.

2 To make the green mayo, place the mayonnaise, parsley, cucumber, and scallions in a bowl and mix together. Cover and chill until required.

3 Preheat the barbecue. Brush the burgers lightly with oil and cook over hot coals for 5–6 minutes on each side, or until piping hot. Serve in hamburger buns with the green mayo.

sweet potato & provolone burgers

ingredients

SERVES 4–6

1 lb/450 g sweet potatoes,
  peeled and cut into chunks
6 oz/175 g broccoli florets
2–3 garlic cloves, crushed
1 red onion, finely chopped
  or grated
$1^{1}/_{2}$–2 fresh red jalapeño
  chiles, seeded and finely
  chopped
6 oz/175 g provolone cheese,
  grated
2 tbsp whole-wheat flour
2–3 tbsp corn oil
1 lb/450 g onions, sliced
1 tbsp chopped fresh cilantro
salt and pepper
hamburger buns, to serve
salad greens, to serve

method

1 Cook the sweet potato in a pan of lightly salted boiling water for 15–20 minutes, or until tender. Drain and mash. Cut the broccoli into small pieces, cook in a separate pan of boiling water for 3 minutes, then drain and plunge into cold water. Drain again, then add to the mashed sweet potato.

2 Stir in the garlic, red onion, chile, grated cheese, and salt and pepper. Mix well and shape into 4–6 equal-size burgers, then coat in the flour. Cover and let chill for at least 1 hour.

3 Heat $1^{1}/_{2}$ tablespoons of the oil in a heavy-bottom skillet. Add the onions with any remaining chile and cook over medium heat for 12–15 minutes, or until softened. Stir in the cilantro and set aside.

4 Preheat the barbecue. When hot, lightly brush the burgers with the remaining oil and cook over hot coals for 5–6 minutes on each side, or until cooked through. Serve the burgers and onions in hamburger buns with salad greens.

vegetarian chile burgers

ingredients

SERVES 4–6

$^1/_2$ cup bulgur wheat

$10^1/_2$ oz/300 g canned red kidney beans, drained and rinsed

$10^1/_2$ oz/300 g canned cannellini beans, drained

1–2 fresh red jalapeño chiles, seeded and coarsely chopped

2–3 garlic cloves

6 scallions, coarsely chopped

1 yellow bell pepper, seeded, peeled, and chopped

1 tbsp chopped fresh cilantro

1 cup grated sharp cheddar cheese

2 tbsp whole-wheat flour

1–2 tbsp corn oil

1 large tomato, sliced

salt and pepper

hamburger buns, to serve

method

1 Cook the bulgur wheat in a pan of lightly salted water for 12 minutes, or until cooked. Drain and set aside.

2 Place the beans in a food processor with the chiles, garlic, scallions, bell pepper, cilantro, and half the cheese. Using the pulse button, chop finely. Add to the cooked bulgur wheat with salt and pepper to taste. Mix well, then shape into 4–6 equal-size burgers. Cover and let chill for 1 hour. Coat the burgers in the flour.

3 Preheat the barbecue. When hot, lightly brush the burgers with oil and cook over hot coals for 4–6 minutes on each side, or until cooked through. Place 1–2 slices of tomato on top of each burger and sprinkle with the remaining cheese. Cook for a further 2–3 minutes, or until the cheese starts to melt. Serve the burgers in hamburger buns.

mushroom burgers

ingredients

SERVES 4

4 oz/115 g button mushrooms

1 carrot

1 onion

1 zucchini

2 tsp corn oil, plus extra for
    brushing

$1/4$ cup peanuts

2 cups fresh white
    breadcrumbs

1 tbsp chopped fresh parsley

1 tsp yeast extract

1 tbsp all-purpose flour,
    for dusting

salt and pepper

method

1 Using a sharp knife, finely chop the mushrooms, then chop the carrot, onion, and zucchini, and set aside. Heat the oil in a heavy-bottom skillet, add the mushrooms, and cook, stirring, for 8 minutes, or until all the moisture has evaporated. Using a slotted spoon, transfer the cooked mushrooms to a large bowl.

2 Put the carrot, onion, zucchini, and peanuts into a food processor and process until finely chopped. Transfer to the bowl containing the mushrooms and stir in the breadcrumbs, chopped parsley, and yeast extract. Season to taste with salt and pepper. Lightly flour your hands and form the mixture into 4 burgers. Place on a large plate, cover with plastic wrap, and let chill in the refrigerator for at least 1 hour and up to 1 day.

3 Preheat the barbecue. Brush the mushroom burgers with the corn oil and cook over hot coals for 8–10 minutes. Serve.

bleu cheese & apple burgers

ingredients

SERVES 4–6

6 oz/175 g new potatoes

scant 1¹/₂ cups mixed nuts,
  such as pecans, almonds,
  and hazelnuts

1 onion, coarsely chopped

8 oz/225 g apples, peeled,
  cored and chopped

6 oz/175 g bleu cheese
  crumbled

1 cup fresh whole-wheat
  breadcrumbs

2 tbsp whole-wheat flour

1–2 tbsp corn oil

salt and pepper

to serve

hamburger buns

salad greens

red onion slices

method

1 Cook the potatoes in a pan of boiling water for 15–20 minutes, or until tender when pierced with a fork. Drain and, using a potato masher, crush into small pieces. Place in a large bowl.

2 Place the nuts and onion in a food processor and, using the pulse button, chop finely. Add the nuts, onion, apple, cheese, and breadcrumbs to the potatoes in the bowl. Season with salt and pepper to taste. Mix well, then shape into 4–6 equal-size burgers. Coat in the flour, then cover and let chill for 1 hour.

3 Preheat the barbecue. When hot, lightly brush the burgers with the oil and cook over hot coals for 5–6 minutes on each side, or until cooked through. Serve the burgers in hamburger buns with salad greens and red onion slices.

butternut squash & polenta burgers

ingredients

SERVES 4–6

1 lb/450 g butternut squash
   (8 oz/225 g after peeling
   and seeding), cut
   into chunks

²/₃ cup water

generous ¹/₂ cup instant
   polenta

4 oz/115 g celeriac, peeled
   and grated

6 scallions, finely chopped

1 cup pecans, chopped

¹/₂ cup freshly grated
   Parmesan cheese

2 tbsp chopped fresh mixed
   herbs

2 tbsp whole-wheat flour

2 tbsp corn oil

salt and pepper

to serve

hamburger buns
salad greens
tomato slices
French fries

method

1 Cook the butternut squash in a pan of boiling water for 15–20 minutes, or until tender. Drain and finely chop or mash. Place the water in a separate pan and bring to a boil. Slowly pour in the polenta in a steady stream and cook over gentle heat, stirring, for 5 minutes, or until thick.

2 Remove the pan from the heat and stir in the butternut squash, celeriac, scallions, pecans, cheese, herbs, and salt and pepper to taste. Mix well, then shape into 4–6 equal-size burgers. Cover and let chill for at least 1 hour. Coat the burgers lightly in the flour.

3 Preheat the barbecue. When hot, lightly brush the burgers with oil and cook over hot coals for 5–6 minutes on each side, or until cooked through. Serve the burgers in hamburger buns with salad greens and tomato slices, and French fries on the side.

vegetable & tofu burgers

ingredients

SERVES 4–6

generous $^1/_2$ cup Thai rice

4 oz/115 g carrot, grated

6 scallions, coarsely chopped

scant $^1/_2$ cup unsalted
    peanuts

generous $^1/_2$ cup fresh bean
    sprouts

8 oz/225 g firm tofu (drained
    weight), finely chopped

1 tsp prepared ginger pulp

$^1/_2$–1 tsp crushed chile

1–2 tbsp corn oil

to serve

hamburger buns

salad greens

fried mushrooms

relish

method

1 Cook the rice in a pan of lightly boiling water for 12–15 minutes, or until soft. Drain and place in a large bowl.

2 Place the carrot, scallions, and peanuts in a food processor and, using the pulse button, chop finely. Add the rice, bean sprouts, tofu, ginger, and chile and blend together. Shape into 4–6 equal-size burgers, firmly pressing them together. Cover and let chill for 1 hour.

3 Preheat the barbecue. When hot, lightly brush the burgers with the oil and cook over hot coals for 5–6 minutes on each side, or until cooked through. Serve the burgers in hamburger buns with salad greens, fried mushrooms and relish.

family favorites

The sun's shining, the cover's off the barbecue, and now you must make the decision of what to cook. Everyone has their own special favorite but there are some recipes that are always popular with all the family. Meat is many people's first choice, whether sizzling steaks, spicy ribs, succulent chops, or scrumptious sausages. Kids, in particular, love chicken, especially if they can eat it with their fingers—the stickier they get, the more fun they have. Even adults enjoy nibbling on spicy wings or marinated drumsticks.

Fish lovers will stake a claim for salmon and tuna, both of them ideal for barbecue grilling and absolutely delicious served with a fresh salsa. Less robust fish are great cooked in packages and there's something specially appetizing about unwrapping it on your plate to release the aromas and reveal the finished dish.

Vegetarian sausages are perennially popular with those who don't eat meat and when they are homemade, they are a real treat. On the other hand, cheese, vegetables, and a barbecue go together so naturally that even meat lovers will want to share these vegetarian delights.

There's only one problem with this abundance of family favorites—you are so spoiled for choice, how can you decide which to cook first?

barbecued steak fajitas

ingredients

SERVES 4

2 tbsp corn oil, plus extra
    for oiling

finely grated rind of 1 lime

1 tbsp lime juice

2 garlic cloves, crushed

$1/4$ tsp ground coriander

$1/4$ tsp ground cumin

pinch of sugar

1 piece of sirloin or top round,
    about 1 lb 8 oz/675 g and
    $3/4$ inch/2 cm thick

4 flour tortillas

1 avocado

2 tomatoes, thinly sliced

4 tbsp sour cream

4 scallions, thinly sliced

salt and pepper

method

1 To make the marinade, put the oil, lime rind and juice, garlic, coriander, cumin, sugar, and salt and pepper to taste into a shallow, nonmetallic dish large enough to hold the steak and mix together. Add the steak and turn in the marinade to coat it. Cover and let marinate in the refrigerator for 6–8 hours or up to 24 hours, turning occasionally.

2 When ready to cook, preheat the barbecue. Using a slotted spoon, remove the steak from the marinade, put onto the grill rack, and cook over medium heat for 5 minutes for rare or 8–10 minutes for medium, turning the steak frequently and basting once or twice with any remaining marinade.

3 Meanwhile, warm the tortillas according to the instructions on the package. Peel, pit, and slice the avocado.

4 Thinly slice the steak across the grain and arrange an equal quantity of the slices on one side of each tortilla. Add the tomato and avocado slices, top with a spoonful of sour cream, and sprinkle over the scallions. Fold over and eat at once.

boozy beef steaks

ingredients

SERVES 4

4 beef steaks

4 tbsp whiskey or brandy

2 tbsp soy sauce

1 tbsp dark brown sugar

tomato slices

pepper

fresh parsley sprigs,
    to garnish

garlic bread, to serve

method

1 Make a few cuts in the edge of the fat on each steak. This will stop the meat from curling as it cooks. Place the meat in a shallow, nonmetallic dish.

2 Mix the whiskey, soy sauce, sugar, and pepper to taste together in a small bowl, stirring until the sugar dissolves. Pour the mixture over the steak. Cover with plastic wrap and let marinate in the refrigerator for at least 2 hours.

3 Preheat the barbecue. Cook the beef steaks over hot coals, searing the meat over the hottest part of the grill for 2 minutes on each side.

4 Move the meat to an area with slightly less intense heat and cook for an additional 4–10 minutes on each side, depending on how well done you like your steaks. To test if the meat is cooked, insert the point of a sharp knife into the meat—the juices will run from red when the meat is still rare, to clear as it becomes well cooked.

5 Lightly grill the tomato slices for 1–2 minutes. Transfer the meat and the tomatoes to warmed serving plates. Garnish with fresh parsley sprigs and serve with garlic bread.

meatballs on sticks

ingredients

SERVES 8

4 pork and herb sausages

$1/2$ cup fresh ground beef

$1^1/2$ cups fresh white
breadcrumbs

1 onion, finely chopped

2 tbsp chopped mixed fresh
herbs, such as parsley,
thyme, and sage

1 egg

salt and pepper

corn oil, for brushing

sauces of your choice,
to serve

method

1 Preheat the barbecue. Remove the sausage meat from the skins, place in a large bowl, and break up with a fork. Add the ground beef, breadcrumbs, onion, herbs, and egg. Season to taste with salt and pepper and stir well with a wooden spoon until thoroughly mixed.

2 Form the mixture into small balls, about the size of a golf ball, between the palms of your hands. Spear each one with a toothpick and brush with oil.

3 Cook over medium hot coals, turning frequently and brushing with more oil as necessary, for 10 minutes, or until cooked through. Transfer to a large serving plate and serve immediately with a choice of sauces.

barbecued pork sausages with thyme

ingredients

SERVES 4

1 garlic clove, finely chopped

1 onion, grated

1 small red chile, seeded and
    finely chopped

1 lb/450 g lean ground pork

scant ⅔ cup almonds,
    toasted and ground

1 cup fresh breadcrumbs

1 tbsp finely chopped fresh
    thyme

salt and pepper

flour, for dusting

vegetable oil, for brushing

to serve

fresh hot-dog rolls

onion slices, lightly cooked

ketchup

method

1 Put the garlic, onion, chile, pork, almonds, breadcrumbs, and thyme into a large bowl. Season well with salt and pepper and mix until well combined.

2 Using your hands, form the mixture into sausage shapes. Roll each sausage in a little flour, then transfer to a bowl, cover with plastic wrap, and let chill for 45 minutes.

3 Preheat the barbecue. Brush a piece of aluminum foil with oil, then put the sausages on the foil and brush them with a little more vegetable oil. Transfer the sausages and foil to the barbecue.

4 Barbecue over hot coals, turning the sausages frequently, for about 15 minutes, or until cooked through. Serve with hot-dog rolls, cooked sliced onion, and ketchup.

hot & spicy pork ribs

ingredients

SERVES 4

1 onion, chopped

2 garlic cloves, chopped

1-inch/2.5-cm piece fresh
    ginger, sliced

1 fresh red chile, seeded and
    chopped

5 tbsp dark soy sauce

3 tbsp lime juice

1 tbsp brown sugar

2 tbsp peanut oil

2 lb 4 oz/1 kg pork spareribs,
    separated

salt and pepper

few springs of flat-leaf parsley,
    to garnish

method

1 Preheat the barbecue. Put the onion, garlic, ginger, chile, and soy sauce into a food processor and process to a paste. Transfer to a measuring cup and stir in the lime juice, sugar, and oil. Season with salt and pepper.

2 Place the spareribs in a preheated wok or large, heavy-bottom pan and pour in the soy sauce mixture. Place on the stove and bring to a boil, then let simmer over low heat, stirring frequently, for 30 minutes. If the mixture appears to be drying out, add a little water.

3 Remove the spareribs, reserving the sauce. Cook the ribs over medium hot coals, turning and basting frequently with the sauce, for 20–30 minutes. Transfer to a large serving plate, garnish with a few sprigs of parsley, and serve immediately.

honey-glazed pork chops

ingredients

SERVES 4

4 lean pork loin chops

4 tbsp clear honey

1 tbsp dry sherry

4 tbsp orange juice

2 tbsp olive oil

1-inch/2.5-cm piece fresh
    ginger, grated

salt and pepper

corn oil, for oiling

method

1 Preheat the barbecue. Season the pork chops with salt and pepper to taste. Reserve while you make the glaze.

2 To make the glaze, place the honey, sherry, orange juice, olive oil, and ginger in a small pan and heat gently, stirring constantly, until well blended.

3 Cook the pork chops on an oiled rack over hot coals for 5 minutes on each side.

4 Brush the chops with the glaze and cook for an additional 2–4 minutes on each side, basting frequently with the glaze.

5 Transfer the pork chops to warmed serving plates and serve hot.

minted lamb chops

ingredients

SERVES 6

6 lamb chops, about
    6 oz/175 g each

2/3 cup strained plain yogurt

2 garlic cloves, finely
    chopped

1 tsp grated fresh ginger

1/4 tsp coriander seeds,
    crushed

1 tbsp olive oil, plus extra
    for brushing

1 tbsp orange juice

1 tsp walnut oil

2 tbsp chopped fresh mint

salt and pepper

method

1 Place the chops in a large, shallow, nonmetallic bowl. Mix half the yogurt, the garlic, ginger, and coriander seeds together in a measuring cup and season to taste with salt and pepper. Spoon the mixture over the chops, turning to coat, then cover with plastic wrap and let marinate in the refrigerator for 2 hours, turning occasionally.

2 Preheat the barbecue. Place the remaining yogurt, the olive oil, orange juice, walnut oil, and mint in a small bowl and, using a handheld blender, mix until thoroughly blended. Season to taste with salt and pepper. Cover the minted yogurt with plastic wrap and let chill in the refrigerator until ready to serve.

3 Drain the chops, scraping off the marinade. Brush with olive oil and cook over medium hot coals for 5–7 minutes on each side. Serve immediately with the minted yogurt.

spicy lamb steaks

ingredients

SERVES 4

4 lamb steaks, about
    6 oz/175 g each
8 fresh rosemary sprigs
8 fresh bay leaves
2 tbsp olive oil
French bread, to serve

spicy marinade

2 tbsp corn oil
1 large onion, finely chopped
2 garlic cloves, finely chopped
2 tbsp Jamaican jerk
    seasoning
1 tbsp curry paste
1 tsp grated fresh ginger
14 oz/400 g canned chopped
    tomatoes
4 tbsp Worcestershire sauce
3 tbsp light brown sugar
salt and pepper

method

1 To make the marinade, heat the oil in a heavy-bottom pan. Add the onion and garlic and cook, stirring occasionally, for 5 minutes, or until softened. Stir in the jerk seasoning, curry paste, and grated ginger, and cook, stirring constantly, for 2 minutes. Add the tomatoes, Worcestershire sauce, and sugar, then season to taste with salt and pepper. Bring to a boil, stirring constantly, then reduce the heat and let simmer for 15 minutes, or until thickened. Remove from the heat and let cool.

2 Place the lamb steaks between 2 sheets of plastic wrap and beat with the side of a rolling pin to flatten. Transfer the steaks to a large, shallow, nonmetallic dish. Pour the marinade over them, turning to coat. Cover with plastic wrap and let marinate in the refrigerator for 3 hours.

3 Preheat the barbecue. Drain the lamb, reserving the marinade. Cook the lamb over medium hot coals, brushing frequently with the marinade, for 5–7 minutes on each side. Meanwhile, dip the rosemary and bay leaves in the olive oil and cook on the barbecue for 3–5 minutes. Serve the lamb immediately with the herbs and French bread.

spicy chicken wings

ingredients

SERVES 4

16 chicken wings

4 tbsp corn oil

4 tbsp light soy sauce

2-inch/5-cm piece of fresh
  ginger, coarsely chopped

2 garlic cloves, coarsely
  chopped

juice and grated rind of
  1 lemon

2 tsp ground cinnamon

2 tsp ground turmeric

4 tbsp honey

salt and pepper

s a u c e

2 orange bell peppers

2 yellow bell peppers

corn oil, for brushing

$1/2$ cup plain yogurt

2 tbsp dark soy sauce

2 tbsp chopped fresh cilantro,
  plus extra to garnish

method

1 Place the chicken wings in a large, shallow, nonmetallic dish. Put the oil, soy sauce, ginger, garlic, lemon rind and juice, cinnamon, turmeric, and honey into a food processor and process to a smooth puree. Season to taste with salt and pepper. Spoon the mixture over the chicken wings and turn until thoroughly coated, cover with plastic wrap, and let marinate in the refrigerator for up to 8 hours.

2 Preheat the barbecue. To make the sauce, brush the bell peppers with the oil and cook over hot coals, turning frequently, for 10 minutes, or until the skin is blackened and charred. Remove from the barbecue and let cool slightly, then remove the skins and discard the seeds. Put the flesh into a food processor with the yogurt and process to a smooth puree. Transfer to a bowl and stir in the soy sauce and chopped cilantro.

3 Drain the chicken wings, reserving the marinade. Cook over medium hot coals, turning and brushing frequently with the reserved marinade, for 8–10 minutes, or until thoroughly cooked. Serve immediately with the sauce and garnished with fresh cilantro.

jerk chicken

ingredients

SERVES 4

4 lean chicken parts

1 bunch of scallions, trimmed

1–2 chiles (Scotch bonnet,
    if possible)

1 garlic clove

2-inch/5-cm piece of fresh
    ginger, peeled and roughly
    chopped

$^1/_2$ tsp dried thyme

$^1/_2$ tsp paprika

$^1/_4$ tsp ground allspice

pinch ground cinnamon

pinch ground cloves

4 tbsp white wine vinegar

3 tbsp light soy sauce

12 whole, barbecued chiles,
    to serve

pepper

method

1 Rinse the chicken parts and pat them dry on paper towels. Place them in a shallow dish.

2 Place the scallions, chiles, garlic, ginger, thyme, paprika, allspice, cinnamon, cloves, wine vinegar, soy sauce, and pepper to taste in a food processor and process until smooth.

3 Pour the spicy mixture over the chicken. Turn the chicken parts over so that they are well coated in the marinade.

4 Transfer the chicken parts to the refrigerator and let marinate for up to 24 hours.

5 Preheat the barbecue. Remove the chicken from the marinade and grill over medium hot coals for about 30 minutes, turning the chicken over and basting occasionally with any remaining marinade, until the chicken is browned and cooked through.

6 Transfer the chicken parts to individual serving plates and serve with the barbecued, whole chiles.

cajun chicken

ingredients

SERVES 4

4 chicken drumsticks

4 chicken thighs

2 fresh corn cobs, husks and
   silks removed

6 tbsp butter, melted

few sprigs of flat-leaf parsley,
   to garnish

spice mix

2 tsp onion powder

2 tsp paprika

$1^{1}/_{2}$ tsp salt

1 tsp garlic powder

1 tsp dried thyme

1 tsp cayenne pepper

1 tsp ground black pepper

$^{1}/_{2}$ tsp ground white pepper

$^{1}/_{4}$ tsp ground cumin

method

1 Preheat the barbecue. Using a sharp knife, make 2–3 diagonal slashes in the chicken drumsticks and thighs, then place them in a large dish. Cut the corn cobs into thick slices and add them to the dish. Mix all the ingredients for the spice mix together in a small bowl.

2 Brush the chicken and corn with the melted butter and sprinkle with the spice mix. Toss to coat well.

3 Cook the chicken over medium hot coals, turning occasionally, for 15 minutes, then add the corn slices and cook, turning occasionally, for an additional 10–15 minutes, or until starting to blacken slightly at the edges. Transfer to a large serving plate, garnish with some sprigs of parsley, and serve immediately.

mustard & honey chicken drumsticks

ingredients

SERVES 4

8 chicken drumsticks

salad greens, to serve

glaze

$1/2$ cup honey

4 tbsp Dijon mustard

4 tbsp whole-grain mustard

4 tbsp white wine vinegar

2 tbsp corn oil

salt and pepper

method

1 Using a sharp knife, make 2–3 diagonal slashes in the chicken drumsticks and place them in a large, nonmetallic dish.

2 Mix all the ingredients for the glaze together in a measuring cup and season to taste with salt and pepper. Pour the glaze over the drumsticks, turning until the drumsticks are well coated. Cover with plastic wrap and let marinate in the refrigerator for at least 1 hour.

3 Preheat the barbecue. Drain the chicken drumsticks, reserving the marinade. Cook the chicken over medium hot coals, turning frequently and brushing with the reserved marinade, for 25–30 minutes, or until thoroughly cooked. Transfer to serving plates and serve immediately with the salad greens.

spicy pita pockets

ingredients

SERVES 4

1 lb 2 oz/500 g skinless,
    boneless chicken, cut into
    1-inch/2.5-cm cubes
3 tbsp plain yogurt
1 tsp chili powder
3 tbsp lime juice
1 tbsp chopped fresh cilantro
1 fresh green chile, seeded
    and finely chopped
1 tbsp corn oil
salt

sauce

2 tbsp corn oil
1 onion, chopped
2 garlic cloves, crushed
4 large tomatoes, peeled,
    seeded, and chopped
2 fresh red chiles, seeded
    and chopped
pinch of ground cumin
salt and pepper

to serve

4 pita breads
$\frac{1}{4}$ iceberg lettuce, shredded
2 tomatoes, thinly sliced
8 scallions, chopped
1 tbsp lemon juice
8 bottled jalapeño chiles,
    drained

method

1 Place the chicken in a large bowl. Mix the yogurt, chili powder, lime juice, fresh cilantro, green chile, and corn oil together in a measuring cup and season to taste with salt. Pour the mixture over the chicken and turn until the chicken is coated. Cover with plastic wrap and let marinate in the refrigerator for 2 hours.

2 Preheat the barbecue. To make the sauce, heat the oil in a small pan. Add the onion and garlic and cook over low heat, stirring occasionally, for 10 minutes, or until softened and golden. Add the tomatoes, chiles, and cumin, and season to taste with salt and pepper. Let simmer gently for 15 minutes, or until reduced and thickened.

3 Set the pan of sauce on the side of the barbecue to keep warm. Drain the chicken, reserving the marinade. Thread the chicken onto presoaked wooden skewers. Cook over medium hot coals, turning and brushing frequently with the reserved marinade, for 6–10 minutes, or until thoroughly cooked. Meanwhile, slit the pita breads with a sharp knife and toast briefly on the barbecue. Remove the chicken from the skewers and fill the pita breads with lettuce, tomato slices, scallions, and chicken. Sprinkle with lemon juice and top with the bottled chiles. Serve immediately with the sauce.

charred fish

ingredients

SERVES 4

4 white fish steaks
1 tbsp paprika
1 tsp dried thyme
1 tsp cayenne pepper
1 tsp black pepper
$1/2$ tsp white pepper
$1/2$ tsp salt
$1/4$ tsp ground allspice
$3^1/2$ tbsp unsalted butter
3 tbsp corn oil
green beans, to serve

method

1 Preheat the barbecue. Rinse the fish steaks under cold running water and pat dry with paper towels.

2 Mix the paprika, thyme, cayenne, black and white peppers, salt, and ground allspice together in a shallow dish.

3 Place the butter and corn oil in a small pan and heat gently, stirring occasionally, until the butter melts.

4 Brush the butter mixture liberally all over the fish steaks, on both sides, then dip the fish into the spicy mix until coated on both sides.

5 Cook the fish over hot coals for 5 minutes on each side, until cooked through. Continue to baste the fish with the remaining butter mixture during the cooking time. Serve with the green beans.

salmon with mango salsa

ingredients

SERVES 4

4 salmon steaks, about
    6 oz/175 g each
finely grated rind and juice of
    1 lime or $^1/_2$ lemon
salt and pepper

salsa

1 large mango, peeled,
    seeded, and diced
1 red onion, finely chopped
2 passion fruit
2 fresh basil sprigs
2 tbsp lime juice
salt

method

1 Preheat the barbecue. Rinse the salmon steaks under cold running water, pat dry with paper towels, and place in a large, shallow, nonmetallic dish. Sprinkle with the lime rind and pour the juice over them. Season to taste with salt and pepper, cover, and let stand while you make the salsa.

2 Place the mango flesh in a bowl with the onion. Cut the passion fruit in half and scoop out the seeds and pulp with a teaspoon into the bowl. Tear the basil leaves and add them to the bowl with the lime juice. Season to taste with salt and stir. Cover with plastic wrap and set aside until required.

3 Cook the salmon steaks over medium hot coals for 3–4 minutes on each side. Serve immediately with the salsa.

chargrilled tuna with chile salsa

ingredients

SERVES 4

4 tuna steaks, about
    6 oz/175 g each
grated rind and juice of 1 lime
2 tbsp olive oil
salt and pepper
fresh cilantro sprigs,
    to garnish
lettuce leaves, to garnish
crusty bread, to serve

chile salsa

2 orange bell peppers
1 tbsp olive oil
juice of 1 lime
juice of 1 orange
2–3 fresh red chiles, seeded
    and chopped
pinch of cayenne pepper

method

1 Rinse the tuna thoroughly under cold running water and pat dry with paper towels, then place in a large, shallow, nonmetallic dish. Sprinkle with the lime rind and pour the juice and olive oil over the fish. Season to taste with salt and pepper, cover with plastic wrap, and let marinate in the refrigerator for up to 1 hour.

2 Preheat the barbecue. To make the salsa, brush the bell peppers with the olive oil and cook over hot coals, turning frequently, for 10 minutes, or until the skin is blackened and charred. Remove from the barbecue and let cool slightly, then remove the skins and discard the seeds. Put the bell peppers into a food processor with the remaining salsa ingredients and process to a puree. Transfer to a bowl and season to taste with salt and pepper.

3 Cook the tuna over hot coals for 4–5 minutes on each side, until golden. Transfer to serving plates, garnish with cilantro sprigs and lettuce leaves, and serve with the salsa and plenty of crusty bread.

cod & tomato packages

ingredients

SERVES 4

4 cod steaks, about
   6 oz/175 g each
2 tsp extra virgin olive oil
4 tomatoes, peeled and
   chopped
2 tbsp fresh basil leaves,
   torn into small pieces
4 tbsp white wine
salt and pepper

method

1 Preheat the barbecue. Rinse the cod steaks under cold running water and pat dry with paper towels. Using a sharp knife, cut out and discard the central bones. Cut out 4 rectangles, 13 x 8 inches/33 x 20 cm, from double-thickness foil and brush with the olive oil. Place a cod steak in the center of each piece of foil.

2 Mix the tomatoes, basil, and white wine together in a bowl and season to taste with salt and pepper. Spoon the tomato mixture equally on top of the fish. Bring up the sides of the foil and fold over securely.

3 Cook the cod packages over hot coals for 3–5 minutes on each side. Transfer to 4 large serving plates and serve immediately in the packages.

eggplant & mozzarella sandwich

ingredients

SERVES 2

1 large eggplant

1 tbsp lemon juice

3 tbsp olive oil

1¼ cups grated mozzarella
cheese

2 sun-dried tomatoes,
chopped

salt and pepper

to serve

Italian bread

mixed salad greens

tomato slices

method

1 Preheat the barbecue. Using a sharp knife, slice the eggplant into thin circles.

2 Mix the lemon juice and olive oil together in a small bowl and season the mixture with salt and pepper to taste. Brush the eggplant slices with the olive oil and lemon juice mixture and cook over medium hot coals for 2–3 minutes, without turning, until golden on the underside.

3 Turn half of the eggplant slices over and sprinkle with cheese and chopped sun-dried tomatoes.

4 Place the remaining eggplant slices on top of the cheese and tomatoes, turning them so that the pale side is facing up. Cook for 1–2 minutes, then carefully turn the whole sandwich over and cook for an additional 1–2 minutes. Baste with the olive oil mixture.

5 Serve in Italian bread with mixed salad greens and a few slices of tomato.

vegetarian sausages

ingredients

SERVES 4

1 tbsp corn oil, plus extra
    for oiling
1 small onion, finely chopped
2 oz/50 g button mushrooms,
    finely chopped
$^1/_2$ red bell pepper, seeded
    and finely chopped
14 oz/400 g canned
    cannellini beans, rinsed
    and drained
2 cups fresh breadcrumbs
1 cup grated cheddar cheese
1 tsp dried mixed herbs
1 egg yolk
seasoned all-purpose flour

to serve

hot-dog rolls
fried onion slices
tomato chutney

method

1 Heat the corn oil in a pan. Add the onion, mushrooms, and bell pepper, and cook until softened.

2 Mash the cannellini beans in a large bowl. Add the onion, mushroom, and bell pepper mixture, the breadcrumbs, cheese, herbs, and egg yolk and mix well. Press the mixture together with your fingers and shape into 8 sausages. Roll each sausage in the seasoned flour. Chill in the refrigerator for at least 30 minutes.

3 Preheat the barbecue. Cook the sausages on a sheet of oiled aluminum foil set over medium hot coals for 15–20 minutes, turning and basting frequently with oil, until golden. Split the hot-dog rolls down the center and insert a layer of cooked onions. Place the sausages in the rolls and serve with tomato chutney.

cheese & vegetable-filled buns

ingredients

SERVES 4

2 red bell peppers, seeded and cut into quarters

2 zucchini, sliced

1 large onion, cut into rings

$5^1/_2$ oz/150 g baby corn

3 tbsp olive oil

4 large hamburger buns, halved horizontally

1 cup grated firm cheese

sour cream, to serve

method

1 Cook the bell peppers on the barbecue, skin-side down, for 5 minutes, or until the skins are charred. Transfer them to a plastic bag, seal the bag, and set to one side. Brush the zucchini, onion rings, and corn with oil and barbecue over hot coals for 5 minutes, turning them frequently and basting with more oil if necessary.

2 While the vegetables are on the barbecue, take the bottom halves of the hamburger buns, brush the cut sides with oil, and sprinkle over some cheese. Cover with the top halves, then wrap each hamburger bun in foil and transfer them to the barbecue. Warm for 2–4 minutes, just until the cheese starts to melt (do not overcook).

3 While the hamburger buns are warming, take the bell pepper quarters from the bag and remove the skins. Chop the flesh into small pieces and transfer it to a plate with the other vegetables.

4 Transfer the hamburger buns to serving plates and remove the foil. Fill them with the cooked vegetables and sour cream and serve at once.

something different

Everyone likes a change from time to time and if you're having a barbecue party, you may want to treat your guests to something a little different and more imaginative than usual. This doesn't have to mean spending a lot more money or even putting in a great deal more time in preparation.

Marinades make all the difference to foods cooked on the barbecue, whether meat or fish. They add a real depth of flavor, tenderize meat, and help to prevent fish from drying out over the heat. They are also very quick and easy to prepare.

While no one is likely to quarrel with a simple but delicious grilled steak, why not try some more adventurous cuts of meat, such as rack of lamb or butterflied poussins? It's surprisingly easy to prepare these little chickens in this impressive way, but you can always ask your butcher to do it for you. Whole fish on the barbecue grill always looks striking—and tempting—even if they're only little silvery sardines.

For an extra-special and probably unexpected treat, serve a hot dessert. Many fruits are transformed by chargrilling. They also look fabulous threaded onto skewers, and when stuffed or served with a luscious sauce, they simply melt in the mouth.

tabasco steaks with watercress butter

ingredients

SERVES 4

1 bunch watercress

6 tbsp butter, softened

4 porterhouse steaks, about
  8 oz/225 g each

4 tsp Tabasco sauce

salt and pepper

method

1 Preheat the barbecue. Using a sharp knife, finely chop enough watercress to fill 4 tablespoons. Reserve a few watercress leaves for the garnish. Place the butter in a small bowl and beat in the chopped watercress with a fork until fully incorporated. Cover with plastic wrap and let chill in the refrigerator until required. Sprinkle each steak with 1 teaspoon of the Tabasco sauce, rubbing it in well. Season to taste with salt and pepper.

2 Cook the steaks over hot coals for $2^1/_2$ minutes each side for rare, 4 minutes each side for medium, and 6 minutes each side for well done. Transfer to serving plates, garnish with the reserved watercress leaves, and serve immediately, topped with the watercress butter.

beef with wild mushrooms

ingredients

SERVES 4

4 beef steaks

3¹/₂ tbsp butter

1–2 garlic cloves, crushed

5¹/₂ oz/150 g mixed wild
  mushrooms

2 tbsp chopped fresh parsley

to serve

salad greens

cherry tomatoes, halved

method

1 Preheat the barbecue. Place the steaks onto a cutting board and using a sharp knife, cut a pocket into the side of each steak.

2 To make the stuffing, heat the butter in a large skillet. Add the garlic and cook gently for 1 minute. Add the mushrooms to the skillet and cook gently for 4–6 minutes, or until tender. Remove the skillet from the heat and stir in the parsley.

3 Divide the mushroom mixture into 4 and insert a portion into the pocket of each steak. Seal the pocket with a toothpick. If preparing ahead, allow the mixture to cool before stuffing the steaks.

4 Cook the steaks over hot coals, searing the meat over the hottest part of the grill for 2 minutes on each side. Move the steaks to an area with slightly less intense heat and cook for an additional 4–10 minutes on each side, depending on how well done you like your steaks.

5 Transfer the steaks to serving plates and remove the toothpicks. Serve the steaks with salad greens and cherry tomatoes.

butterflied lamb with balsamic vinegar & mint

ingredients

SERVES 4

1 boned leg of lamb, about
　　4 lb/1.8 kg

scant $1/2$ cup balsamic
　　vinegar

grated rind and juice of
　　1 lemon

$2/3$ cup corn oil

4 tbsp chopped fresh mint

2 garlic cloves, crushed

2 tbsp brown sugar

salt and pepper

to serve

grilled vegetables, such as
　　bell peppers and zucchini

black or green olives

method

1 Open out the boned leg of lamb so that its shape resembles a butterfly. Thread 2–3 skewers through the meat to make it easier to turn on the grill.

2 Mix the balsamic vinegar, lemon rind and juice, corn oil, mint, garlic, sugar, and salt and pepper to taste together in a nonmetallic dish that is large enough to hold the lamb. Place the lamb in the dish and turn it over a few times so that the meat is coated on both sides with the marinade. Cover and let marinate in the refrigerator for at least 6 hours, or preferably overnight, turning occasionally.

3 Preheat the barbecue. Remove the lamb from the marinade and reserve the liquid for basting. Place the rack about 6 inches/15 cm above the coals and cook the lamb for 30 minutes on each side, turning once and basting frequently with the marinade.

4 Transfer the lamb to a cutting board and remove the skewers. Cut the lamb into slices across the grain and serve with grilled vegetables and olives.

rack of lamb

ingredients

SERVES 4

4 racks of lamb, each with
    4 chops
2 tbsp extra virgin olive oil
1 tbsp balsamic vinegar
1 tbsp lemon juice
3 tbsp finely chopped fresh
    rosemary
1 small onion, finely chopped
salt and pepper

method

1 Place the racks of lamb in a large, shallow, nonmetallic dish. Place the oil, vinegar, lemon juice, rosemary, and onion in a measuring cup and stir together. Season to taste with salt and pepper.

2 Pour the marinade over the lamb and turn until thoroughly coated. Cover with plastic wrap and let marinate in the refrigerator for 1 hour, turning occasionally.

3 Preheat the barbecue. Drain the racks of lamb, reserving the marinade. Cook over medium hot coals, brushing frequently with the marinade, for 10 minutes on each side. Serve immediately.

caribbean pork

ingredients

SERVES 4

4 pork loin chops

4 tbsp dark brown sugar

4 tbsp orange or pineapple
juice

2 tbsp Jamaican rum

1 tbsp dry unsweetened
coconut

$1/2$ tsp ground cinnamon

mixed salad greens, to serve

coconut rice

generous 1 cup basmati rice

2 cups water

$2/3$ cup coconut milk

4 tbsp raisins

4 tbsp roasted peanuts or
cashew nuts

2 tbsp dry unsweetened
coconut, toasted

salt and pepper

method

1 Trim any excess fat from the pork and place the chops in a shallow, nonmetallic dish. Mix the sugar, fruit juice, rum, coconut, and cinnamon together in a bowl, stirring until the sugar dissolves. Pour the mixture over the pork, cover, and let marinate in the refrigerator for 2 hours, or preferably overnight.

2 Preheat the barbecue. Remove the pork from the marinade, reserving the liquid for basting. Cook over hot coals for 15–20 minutes, basting with the marinade.

3 Meanwhile, make the coconut rice. Rinse the rice under cold running water, place it in a pan with the water and coconut milk, and bring gently to a boil. Stir, cover, and reduce the heat. Simmer gently for 12 minutes, or until the rice is tender and the liquid has been absorbed. Fluff up with a fork.

4 Stir the raisins and nuts into the rice, season to taste with salt and pepper, and sprinkle with the dry unsweetened coconut. Transfer the pork and rice to warmed serving plates and serve immediately with mixed salad greens.

lemon & herb pork scallops

ingredients

SERVES 4

4 pork scallops

2 tbsp corn oil

6 bay leaves, torn into pieces

grated rind and juice of
   2 lemons

$1/2$ cup beer

1 tbsp honey

6 juniper berries, lightly
   crushed

1 crisp apple

salt and pepper

method

1 Place the pork scallops in a large, shallow, nonmetallic dish. Heat the oil in a small, heavy-bottom pan. Add the bay leaves and stir-fry for 1 minute. Stir in the lemon rind and juice, beer, honey, and juniper berries, and season to taste with salt and pepper.

2 Pour the mixture over the pork, turning to coat. Cover with plastic wrap, let cool, then let marinate in the refrigerator for up to 8 hours.

3 Preheat the barbecue. Drain the pork, reserving the marinade. Core the apple and cut into rings. Cook the pork over medium hot coals, brushing frequently with the reserved marinade, for 5 minutes on each side, or until thoroughly cooked. Cook the apples on the barbecue, brushing frequently with the marinade, for 3 minutes. Transfer the pork to a large serving plate with the apple rings and serve immediately.

tarragon turkey

ingredients

SERVES 4

4 turkey breasts, about
 6 oz/175 g each

4 tsp whole-grain mustard

8 fresh tarragon sprigs, plus
 extra to garnish

4 smoked Canadian bacon
 slices

salt and pepper

salad greens, to serve

method

1 Preheat the barbecue. Season the turkey to taste with salt and pepper, and, using a round-bladed knife, spread the mustard evenly over the turkey.

2 Place 2 tarragon sprigs on top of each turkey breast and wrap a bacon slice around it to hold the herbs in place. Secure with a toothpick.

3 Cook the turkey over medium hot coals for 5–8 minutes on each side. Transfer to serving plates and garnish with tarragon sprigs. Serve with salad greens.

butterflied poussins

ingredients

SERVES 4

4 poussins, about 1 lb/450 g
   each
1 tbsp paprika
1 tbsp mustard powder
1 tbsp ground cumin
pinch of cayenne pepper
1 tbsp ketchup
1 tbsp lemon juice
5 tbsp melted butter
salt
fresh cilantro sprigs,
   to garnish
corn on the cob, to serve

method

1 To butterfly the poussins, turn 1 bird breast-side down and, using strong kitchen scissors or poultry shears, cut through the skin and rib cage along both sides of the backbone, from tail to neck. Remove the backbone and turn the bird breast-side up. Press down firmly on the breastbone to flatten. Fold the wingtips underneath. Push a skewer through one wing, the top of the breast, and out of the other wing. Push a second skewer through one thigh, the bottom of the breast, and out through the other thigh. Repeat with the remaining poussins.

2 Mix the paprika, mustard powder, cumin, cayenne, ketchup, and lemon juice together in a small bowl and season to taste with salt. Gradually stir in the butter to make a smooth paste. Spread the paste evenly over the poussins, cover, and let marinate in the refrigerator for up to 8 hours.

3 Preheat the barbecue. Cook the poussins over medium hot coals, turning frequently, for 25–30 minutes, brushing with a little oil if necessary. Transfer to a serving plate, garnish with fresh cilantro sprigs, and serve with corn on the cob.

fruity duck

ingredients

SERVES 4

4 duck breasts

2/3 cup dried apricots

2 shallots, thinly sliced

2 tbsp honey

1 tsp sesame oil

2 tsp Chinese five-spice
   powder

method

1 Preheat the barbecue. Using a sharp knife, cut a long slit in the fleshy side of each duck breast to make a pocket. Divide the apricots and shallots among the pockets and secure with skewers.

2 Mix the honey and sesame oil together in a small bowl and brush all over the duck. Sprinkle with the Chinese five-spice powder.

3 Cook the duck over medium hot coals for 6–8 minutes on each side. Remove the skewers, transfer to a large serving plate, and serve immediately.

orange & lemon peppered monkfish

ingredients

SERVES 8

2 oranges

2 lemons

2 monkfish tails, about
   1 lb 2 oz/500 g each,
   skinned and cut into
   4 fillets

8 fresh lemon thyme sprigs

2 tbsp olive oil

2 tbsp green peppercorns,
   lightly crushed

salt

method

1 Cut 8 orange slices and 8 lemon slices, reserving the remaining fruit. Rinse the monkfish fillets under cold running water and pat dry with paper towels. Place the monkfish fillets, cut side up, on a counter and divide the citrus slices among them. Top with the lemon thyme. Tie each fillet at intervals with kitchen string to secure the citrus slices and thyme. Place the monkfish in a large, shallow, nonmetallic dish.

2 Squeeze the juice from the remaining fruit and mix with the olive oil in a measuring cup. Season to taste with salt, then spoon the mixture over the fish. Cover with plastic wrap and let marinate in the refrigerator for up to 1 hour, spooning the marinade over the fish tails once or twice.

3 Preheat the barbecue. Drain the monkfish tails, reserving the marinade. Sprinkle the crushed green peppercorns over the fish, pressing them in with your fingers. Cook the monkfish over medium hot coals, turning and brushing frequently with the reserved marinade, for 20–25 minutes. Transfer to a cutting board, remove and discard the string, and cut the monkfish tails into slices. Serve immediately.

chargrilled red snapper

ingredients

SERVES 4

4 banana leaves

2 limes

3 garlic cloves

4 red snappers, about
     12 oz/350 g each

2 scallions, thinly sliced

1-inch/2.5-cm piece fresh
     ginger

1 onion, finely chopped

4^1/$_2$ tsp peanut or corn oil

3 tbsp kecap manis or light
     soy sauce

1 tsp ground coriander

1 tsp ground cumin

^{1}/$_4$ tsp ground cloves

^{1}/$_4$ tsp ground turmeric

method

1 Preheat the barbecue. If necessary, cut the banana leaves into 4 x 16-inch/40-cm squares, using a sharp knife or scissors. Thinly slice 1^1/$_2$ limes and 1 garlic clove. Clean and scale the fish, then rinse it inside and out under cold running water. Pat dry with paper towels. Using a sharp knife, make a series of deep diagonal slashes on the side of each fish, then insert the lime and garlic slices into the slashes. Place the fish on the banana leaf squares and sprinkle with the scallions.

2 Finely chop the remaining garlic and squeeze the juice from the remaining lime half. Finely chop the ginger, then place the garlic in a bowl with the onion, ginger, oil, kecap manis, spices, and lime juice, and mix to a paste.

3 Spoon the paste into the fish cavities and spread it over the outside. Roll up the packages and tie securely with string. Cook over medium hot coals, turning occasionally, for 15–20 minutes. Serve.

shrimp with citrus salsa

ingredients

SERVES 6

36 large, raw jumbo shrimp

2 tbsp finely chopped fresh
    cilantro

pinch of cayenne pepper

3–4 tbsp corn oil

fresh cilantro leaves,
    to garnish

lime wedges, to serve

salsa

1 orange

1 tart apple, peeled,
    quartered, and cored

2 fresh red chiles, seeded
    and chopped

1 garlic clove, chopped

8 fresh cilantro sprigs

8 fresh mint sprigs

4 tbsp lime juice

salt and pepper

method

1 Preheat the barbecue. To make the salsa, peel the orange and cut into segments. Set aside any juice. Put the orange segments, apple quarters, chiles, garlic, cilantro, and mint into a food processor and process until smooth. With the motor running, add the lime juice through the feeder tube. Transfer the salsa to a serving bowl and season to taste with salt and pepper. Cover with plastic wrap and let chill in the refrigerator until required.

2 Using a sharp knife, remove and discard the heads from the shrimp, then remove the shells. Cut along the back of the shrimp and remove the dark intestinal vein. Rinse the shrimp under cold running water and pat dry with paper towels. Mix the chopped cilantro, cayenne, and corn oil together in a dish. Add the shrimp and toss well to coat.

3 Cook the shrimp over medium hot coals for 3 minutes on each side, or until they have changed color. Transfer to a large serving plate, garnish with fresh cilantro leaves, and serve immediately with lime wedges and the salsa.

stuffed sardines

ingredients

SERVES 6

1 tbsp fresh parsley, finely
   chopped
4 garlic cloves, finely
   chopped
12 fresh sardines, cleaned
   and scaled
3 tbsp lemon juice
scant $^2/_3$ cup all-purpose flour
1 tsp ground cumin
salt and pepper
olive oil, for brushing

method

1 Place the parsley and garlic in a bowl and mix together. Rinse the fish inside and out under cold running water and pat dry with paper towels. Spoon the herb mixture into the fish cavities and pat the remainder all over the outside of the fish. Sprinkle the sardines with lemon juice and transfer to a large, shallow, nonmetallic dish. Cover with plastic wrap and let marinate in the refrigerator for 1 hour.

2 Preheat the barbecue. Mix the flour and ground cumin together in a bowl, then season to taste with salt and pepper. Spread out the seasoned flour on a large plate and gently roll the sardines in the flour to coat.

3 Brush the sardines with olive oil and cook over medium hot coals for 3–4 minutes on each side. Serve immediately.

chargrilled devils

ingredients

SERVES 6

36 fresh oysters

18 rindless, lean bacon strips

1 tbsp mild paprika

1 tsp cayenne pepper

sauce

1 fresh red chile, seeded and
finely chopped

1 garlic clove, finely chopped

1 shallot, finely chopped

2 tbsp finely chopped fresh
parsley

2 tbsp lemon juice

salt and pepper

method

1 Preheat the barbecue. Open the oysters, catching the juice from the shells in a bowl. Cut the oysters from the bottom shells, set aside, and tip any remaining juice into the bowl. To make the sauce, add the red chile, garlic, shallot, parsley, and lemon juice to the bowl, then season to taste with salt and pepper and mix well. Cover the bowl with plastic wrap and let chill in the refrigerator until required.

2 Using a sharp knife, cut each bacon strip in half across the center. Season the oysters with paprika and cayenne, then roll each oyster up inside half a bacon strip. Thread 6 wrapped oysters onto each presoaked wooden skewer.

3 Cook over hot coals, turning frequently, for 5 minutes, or until the bacon is well browned and crispy. Transfer to a large serving plate and serve immediately with the sauce.

chocolate rum bananas

ingredients

SERVES 4

1 tbsp butter

8 oz/225 g semisweet or milk
    chocolate

4 large bananas

2 tbsp rum

sour cream, mascarpone
    cheese, or ice cream,
        to serve

grated nutmeg, to decorate

method

1 Take four 10-inch/25-cm squares of aluminum foil and brush them with butter.

2 Grate the chocolate. Make a careful slit lengthwise in the peel of each banana, and open just wide enough to insert the chocolate. Place the grated chocolate inside the bananas, along their lengths, then close them up.

3 Wrap each stuffed banana in a square of foil, then barbecue them over hot coals for about 5–10 minutes, or until the chocolate has melted inside the bananas. Remove from the barbecue, place the bananas on individual serving plates, and pour some rum into each banana.

4 Serve at once with sour cream, mascarpone cheese, or ice cream, topped with nutmeg.

mascarpone peaches

ingredients

SERVES 4

4 peaches

6 oz/175 g mascarpone
   cheese

1$\frac{1}{2}$ oz/40 g pecans or
   walnuts, chopped

1 tsp corn oil

4 tbsp maple syrup

method

1 Cut the peaches in half and remove the pits. If you are preparing this recipe in advance, press the peach halves together and wrap in plastic wrap until required.

2 Mix the mascarpone cheese and pecans together in a bowl until well combined. Let chill in the refrigerator until required. Preheat the barbecue. Brush the peach halves with a little corn oil and place on a rack set over medium hot coals. Cook the peach halves for 5–10 minutes, turning once, until hot.

3 Transfer the peach halves to a serving dish and top with the mascarpone and nut mixture. Drizzle the maple syrup over the peaches and mascarpone filling and serve immediately.

tropical pineapple

ingredients

SERVES 4

1 pineapple

3 tbsp dark rum

2 tbsp brown sugar

1 tsp ground ginger

4 tbsp unsalted butter, melted

method

1 Preheat the barbecue. Using a sharp knife, cut off the crown of the pineapple, then cut the fruit into 3/4-inch/2-cm thick slices. Cut away the peel from each slice and flick out the "eyes" with the tip of the knife. Stamp out the cores with an apple corer or small cookie cutter.

2 Mix the rum, sugar, ginger, and butter together in a measuring cup, stirring constantly, until the sugar has dissolved. Brush the pineapple rings with the rum mixture.

3 Cook the pineapple rings over hot coals for 3–4 minutes on each side. Transfer to serving plates and serve immediately with the remaining rum mixture poured over them.

stuffed figs

ingredients

SERVES 4

8 fresh figs

scant $^1/_2$ cup cream cheese

1 tsp ground cinnamon

3 tbsp brown sugar

plain yogurt, sour cream,
mascarpone cheese,
or ice cream, to serve

method

1 Cut out eight 7-inch/18-cm squares of aluminum foil. Make a small cross in each fig, then place each fig on a square of foil.

2 Put the cream cheese in a bowl. Add the cinnamon and stir until well combined. Stuff the inside of each fig with the cinnamon cream cheese, then sprinkle a teaspoon of sugar over each one. Close the foil around each fig to make a package.

3 Place the packages on the barbecue and cook over hot coals, turning them frequently, for about 10 minutes, or until the figs are cooked to your taste.

4 Transfer the figs to serving plates and serve at once with plain yogurt, sour cream, mascarpone cheese, or ice cream.

mixed fruit kabobs

ingredients

SERVES 4

2 nectarines, halved and
    pitted

2 kiwis

4 red plums

1 mango, peeled, halved,
    and pitted

2 bananas, peeled and thickly
    sliced

8 strawberries, hulled

1 tbsp honey

3 tbsp Cointreau

method

1 Cut the nectarine halves into wedges and place in a large, shallow dish. Peel and quarter the kiwis. Cut the plums in half and remove the pits. Cut the mango flesh into chunks and add to the dish with the kiwis, plums, bananas, and strawberries.

2 Mix the honey and Cointreau together in a measuring cup until blended. Pour the mixture over the fruit and toss to coat. Cover with plastic wrap and let marinate in the refrigerator for 1 hour.

3 Preheat the barbecue. Drain the fruit, reserving the marinade. Thread the fruit onto several presoaked wooden skewers and cook over medium hot coals, turning and brushing frequently with the reserved marinade, for 5–7 minutes, then serve.

toffee fruit kabobs

ingredients

SERVES 4

2 apples, cored and cut into wedges

2 firm pears, cored and cut into wedges

juice of $1/2$ lemon

2 tbsp brown sugar

2 tbsp ground allspice

generous $1/2$ cup butter, melted

sauce

$4^1/2$ oz/125 g butter

$1/2$ cup brown sugar

6 tbsp heavy cream

method

1 Preheat the barbecue. Toss the apples and pears in the lemon juice to prevent any discoloration.

2 Mix the sugar and allspice together and sprinkle over the fruit. Thread the fruit pieces onto skewers.

3 To make the toffee sauce, place the butter and sugar in a pan and heat, stirring gently, until the butter has melted and the sugar has dissolved.

4 Add the cream to the pan and bring to a boil. Boil for 1–2 minutes, then let cool slightly.

5 Meanwhile, place the fruit kabobs over hot coals and cook for 5 minutes, turning and basting frequently with the melted butter, until the fruit is just tender. Transfer the fruit kabobs to warmed serving plates and serve with the cooled toffee sauce.

skewers

Whether they're called kabobs, brochettes, or any other name, bite-size pieces of meat, fish, and vegetables threaded onto skewers and sizzling on the barbecue grill always look appetizing and appealing. They are ideal for entertaining because they seem special and, although they can be time consuming to prepare, they cook very quickly. This is especially helpful if your barbecue isn't very big and you have a lot of guests. Children absolutely love kabobs, but make sure that you transfer the food for them before serving it—you don't want small mouths burned on hot metal or tongues impaled on the pointed ends of skewers.

Shrimp are "custom-made" for kabobs, and cubes of meaty fish, such as swordfish, cheese, firm tofu, and vegetables are also ideal because they taste best when cooked quickly. Use good-quality cuts of meat, such as sirloin, tenderloin, and chicken breast portions, and cut them into equal-size cubes. If they are threaded alternately with vegetables or mushrooms, try to make sure that these are the same size too, and don't pack them too tightly or too close to the ends of the skewers.

If you soak bamboo or wooden skewers in cold water for 30 minutes before you use them, this helps to reduce the chances of their charring during cooking.

beef teriyaki

ingredients

SERVES 4

1 lb/450 g extra-thin beef
  steaks
1 yellow bell pepper, seeded
  and cut into chunks
8 scallions, trimmed and cut
  into short lengths
salad greens, to serve

sauce

1 tsp cornstarch
2 tbsp dry sherry
2 tbsp white wine vinegar
3 tbsp soy sauce
1 tbsp dark brown sugar
1 garlic clove, crushed
$1/2$ tsp ground cinnamon
$1/2$ tsp ground ginger

method

1 Place the beef steaks in a shallow, nonmetallic dish. To make the sauce, mix the cornstarch and sherry together in a small bowl, then stir in the remaining sauce ingredients. Pour the sauce over the meat, cover with plastic wrap, and let marinate in the refrigerator for at least 2 hours.

2 Preheat the barbecue. Remove the meat from the sauce and reserve. Pour the sauce into a small pan and cook for at least 5 minutes, stirring occasionally.

3 Cut the meat into thin strips and thread these, concertina-style, onto several presoaked wooden skewers, alternating each strip of meat with the pieces of bell pepper and scallion. Cook the kabobs over hot coals for 5–8 minutes, turning and basting the beef and vegetables occasionally with the reserved sauce.

4 Arrange the skewers on serving plates, pour over the remaining sauce, and serve with salad greens.

surf 'n' turf skewers

ingredients

SERVES 2

8 oz/225 g beef tenderloin,
   about 1 inch/2.5 cm thick

8 raw jumbo shrimp, in their
   shells

4 tbsp butter

2 garlic cloves, crushed

3 tbsp chopped fresh parsley,
   plus extra parsley sprigs,
   to garnish

finely grated rind and juice of
   1 lime

olive oil, for oiling

salt and pepper

lime wedges, to garnish

crusty bread, to serve

method

1 Cut the steak into 1-inch/2.5-cm cubes. To prepare the shrimp, pull off their heads with your fingers, then peel off their shells, leaving the tails on. Using a sharp knife, make a shallow slit along the back of each shrimp, then pull out the dark vein and discard. Rinse the shrimp under cold running water and dry well on paper towels.

2 Thread an equal number of the steak cubes and shrimp onto 2 oiled metal kabob skewers or presoaked wooden skewers. Season the kabobs to taste with pepper.

3 Preheat the barbecue. Meanwhile, put the butter and garlic into a small pan and heat gently until melted. Remove from the heat and add the parsley, lime rind and juice, and salt and pepper to taste. Let stand in a warm place so that the butter remains melted.

4 Brush the kabobs with a little of the melted butter, place on an oiled rack and cook over medium coals for 4–8 minutes, turning frequently or until the steak is cooked to personal preference, and the shrimps turn pink. Brush frequently during cooking with the remaining melted butter.

5 Serve the kabobs hot on the skewers, with the remaining butter spooned over. Garnish with lime wedges and parsley sprigs and serve with crusty bread to mop up the buttery juices.

pork & apple skewers

ingredients

SERVES 4

1 lb/450 g pork tenderloin

1¼ cups hard cider

1 tbsp finely chopped fresh
   sage

6 black peppercorns, crushed

2 crisp apples

1 tbsp corn oil

crusty bread, to serve

method

1 Using a sharp knife, cut the pork into 1-inch/2.5-cm cubes, then place in a large, shallow, nonmetallic dish. Mix the cider, sage, and peppercorns together in a measuring cup, pour the mixture over the pork, and turn until thoroughly coated. Cover and let marinate in the refrigerator for 1–2 hours.

2 Preheat the barbecue. Drain the pork, reserving the marinade. Core the apples, but do not peel, then cut into wedges. Dip the apple wedges into the reserved marinade and thread onto several metal skewers, alternating with the cubes of pork. Stir the corn oil into the remaining marinade.

3 Cook the brochettes over medium hot coals, turning and brushing frequently with the reserved marinade, for 12–15 minutes. Transfer to a large serving plate and if you prefer, remove the meat and apples from the skewers before serving. Serve immediately with crusty bread.

pork & sage kabobs

ingredients

SERVES 4

1 lb/450 g ground pork

$^1/_2$ cup fresh breadcrumbs

1 small onion, very finely
    chopped

1 tbsp fresh sage, chopped

2 tbsp applesauce

$^1/_4$ tsp ground nutmeg

salt and pepper

baste

3 tbsp olive oil

1 tbsp lemon juice

to serve

4 small pita breads

mixed salad greens

6 tbsp thick plain yogurt

method

1 Place the pork in a mixing bowl, together with the breadcrumbs, onion, sage, applesauce, nutmeg, and salt and pepper to taste. Mix until the ingredients are well combined.

2 Using your hands, shape the mixture into small balls, about the size of large marbles, and chill in the refrigerator for at least 30 minutes.

3 Meanwhile, soak several small wooden skewers in cold water for at least 30 minutes. Thread the meatballs onto the skewers.

4 To make the baste, mix together the oil and lemon juice in a small bowl, whisking with a fork until it is well blended.

5 Cook the kabobs over hot coals for 8–10 minutes, turning and basting frequently with the lemon and oil mixture, until the meat is golden and cooked through.

6 Line the pita breads with the salad greens and spoon some of the yogurt on top. Serve with the kabobs.

shish kabobs

ingredients

SERVES 4–6

1 lb 2 oz/500 g boneless leg
   or neck of lamb with a
   small amount of fat, cut
   into 3/4-inch/2-cm cubes
corn oil, for brushing
2 green bell peppers, halved,
   seeded, and cut into
   3/4-inch/2-cm pieces
1 onion, quartered and
   separated into layers
2 cherry tomatoes per skewer
sea salt

marinade

2 tbsp milk
2 tbsp olive oil, plus extra for
   oiling
1 large onion, grated
1 tbsp tomato paste
1/2 tsp ground cumin
coarse sea salt and pepper

to serve

lemon wedges
warmed pita bread (optional)
Tzatziki

method

1 To make the marinade, put all the ingredients in a bowl and stir until the tomato paste is evenly dispersed. Add the lamb cubes and use your hands to coat well with the marinade. Cover and let marinate in the refrigerator for 2 hours. If you are using wooden skewers, soak them in cold water for at least 1 hour.

2 Preheat the barbecue. Lightly brush presoaked wooden or long, flat metal skewers with oil, then thread an equal quantity of the lamb cubes onto each one, occasionally interspersing with green bell pepper pieces, onions layers, and the cherry tomatoes. Sprinkle with sea salt.

3 Place the kabobs on an oiled rack and cook over hot coals, turning frequently and basting with the remaining marinade, for 8–10 minutes, or until the lamb and peppers are charred on the edges.

4 Using a folded cloth to protect your fingers, hold the top of each skewer and use a fork to push the ingredients onto a serving platter. Serve immediately with lemon wedges for squeezing over, warmed pita bread, if using, and Tzatziki.

indian kofta

ingredients

SERVES 4

1 small onion

1 lb/450 g fresh, lean ground lamb

2 tbsp curry paste

2 tbsp plain yogurt

corn oil, for basting

tomato sambal

3 tomatoes, seeded and diced

pinch of ground coriander

pinch of ground cumin

2 tsp chopped fresh cilantro

salt and pepper

to serve

pappadams

chutney

method

1 Place the onion in a food processor and chop finely. Add the lamb and process briefly to chop further. Chopping the meat again will help the kofta mixture to hold together during cooking. Alternatively, grate the onion finely before mixing it with the lamb.

2 Add the curry paste and yogurt and mix well. Divide the mixture into 8 equal-size portions. Press and shape the mixture into 8 sausage shapes and push each one onto a metal or presoaked wooden skewer, pressing the mixture together firmly so that it holds its shape. Let chill in the refrigerator for at least 30 minutes, or until required.

3 To make the tomato sambal, mix the tomatoes, spices, chopped cilantro, and salt and pepper to taste together in a bowl. Let stand for at least 30 minutes for the flavors to combine.

4 Preheat the barbecue. Cook the kabobs on an oiled rack over hot coals for 10–15 minutes, turning frequently. Baste with a little corn oil if needed. Serve accompanied with pappadams, chutney, and tomato sambal.

shashlik

ingredients

SERVES 4

1 lb 8 oz/675 g boneless leg
   of lamb, cut into 1-inch/
   2.5-cm cubes
12 button mushrooms
4 rindless lean bacon strips
8 cherry tomatoes
1 large green bell pepper,
   seeded and cut into
   squares
crusty bread, to serve

marinade

4 tbsp corn oil
4 tbsp lemon juice
1 onion, finely chopped
$^1/_2$ tsp dried rosemary
$^1/_2$ tsp dried thyme
salt and pepper

method

1 Place the lamb and mushrooms in a large, shallow, nonmetallic dish. Mix all the ingredients for the marinade together in a measuring cup, seasoning to taste with salt and pepper. Pour the mixture over the lamb and mushrooms, turning to coat. Cover with plastic wrap and let marinate in the refrigerator for up to 8 hours.

2 Preheat the barbecue. Cut the bacon strips in half across the center and stretch with a heavy, flat-bladed knife, then roll up. Drain the lamb and mushrooms, reserving the marinade. Thread the bacon rolls, lamb, mushrooms, tomatoes, and bell pepper squares alternately onto metal skewers. Strain the marinade.

3 Cook the kabobs over medium hot coals, turning and brushing frequently with the reserved marinade, for 10–15 minutes. Transfer to a large serving plate and serve immediately with crusty bread.

marinated lamb & vegetable kabobs

ingredients

SERVES 4

juice of 2 large lemons

$^1/_3$ cup olive oil

1 garlic clove, crushed

1 tbsp chopped fresh oregano
    or mint

1 lb 9 oz/700 g boned leg or
    fillet of lamb

2 green bell peppers

2 zucchini

12 pearl onions

8 large bay leaves

salt and pepper

Tzatzíki, to serve

method

1 Put the lemon juice, oil, garlic, oregano, salt and pepper in a bowl and whisk together. Trim and cut the lamb into 1$^1/_2$-inch/4-cm cubes and add to the marinade.

2 Toss the lamb in the marinade, cover, and refrigerate overnight or for at least 8 hours. Stir occasionally to coat the lamb.

3 Preheat the barbecue. Core and deseed the bell peppers, and cut into 1$^1/_4$-inch/3-cm cubes. Cut the zucchini into 1-inch/2.5-cm pieces. Thread the lamb, bell peppers, zucchini, onions, and bay leaves onto 8 oiled, flat metal skewers, alternating the ingredients evenly.

4 Place the kabobs on an oiled rack and cook over hot coals for 10–15 minutes, turning frequently and basting with any remaining marinate, until cooked through. Serve hot on a bed of rice, with a bowl of Tzatziki.

chicken satay

ingredients

SERVES 4

8 tbsp crunchy peanut butter

1 onion, coarsely chopped

1 garlic clove, coarsely
   chopped

2 tbsp creamed coconut

4 tbsp peanut oil

1 tsp light soy sauce

2 tbsp lime juice

2 fresh red chiles, seeded
   and chopped

3 kaffir lime leaves, torn

4 skinless, boneless chicken
   breasts, about 6 oz/175 g
   each, cut into 1-inch/
   2.5-cm cubes

method

1 Put the peanut butter, onion, garlic, coconut, peanut oil, soy sauce, lime juice, chiles, and lime leaves into a food processor and process to a smooth paste. Transfer the paste to a large glass bowl.

2 Add the chicken cubes to the dish and stir to coat thoroughly. Cover with plastic wrap and let marinate in the refrigerator for up to 8 hours.

3 Preheat the barbecue. Thread the chicken cubes onto several presoaked wooden skewers, reserving the marinade. Cook the skewers over medium hot coals, turning and brushing frequently with the marinade, for 10 minutes, or until thoroughly cooked. Transfer to a large serving plate and serve immediately.

chicken kabobs with yogurt sauce

ingredients

SERVES 4

1 tbsp chopped fresh herbs
such as oregano, dill,
tarragon, or parsley
4 large skinned, boned
chicken breasts
8 firm stems of fresh
rosemary, optional
corn oil, for brushing
rice, to serve
shredded romaine lettuce,
to serve
lemon wedges, to garnish

sauce

1¼ cups authentic Greek
yogurt, or strained plain
yogurt
2 garlic cloves, crushed
juice of ½ lemon juice
salt and pepper

method

1 To make the sauce, put the yogurt, garlic, lemon juice, oregano, salt and pepper in a large bowl and mix well together.

2 Cut the chicken breasts into chunks measuring about 1½ inches/4 cm square. Add to the yogurt mixture and toss well together until the chicken pieces are coated. Cover and let marinate in the refrigerator for about 1 hour. If you are using wooden skewers, soak them in cold water for 30 minutes.

3 Preheat the barbecue. Thread the pieces of chicken onto 8 flat, presoaked wooden skewers or rosemary stems and place on an oiled rack.

4 Cook the kabobs over hot coals for 15 minutes, turning frequently and basting with the marinade, until lightly browned and tender.

5 Pour the remaining marinade into a saucepan and heat gently but do not boil. Serve the kabobs on a bed of rice topped with shredded lettuce and garnish with lemon wedges. Accompany with the yogurt sauce.

zesty kabobs

ingredients

SERVES 4

4 skinless, boneless chicken
　　breasts, about 6 oz/175 g
　　each
finely grated rind and juice of
　　$1/2$ lemon
finely grated rind and juice of
　　$1/2$ orange
2 tbsp honey
2 tbsp olive oil
2 tbsp chopped fresh mint,
　　plus extra to garnish
$1/4$ tsp ground coriander
salt and pepper
citrus zest, to garnish

method

1 Using a sharp knife, cut the chicken into 1-inch/2.5-cm cubes, then place them in a large glass bowl. Place the lemon and orange rind, the lemon and orange juice, the honey, oil, mint, and ground coriander in a measuring cup and mix together. Season to taste with salt and pepper. Pour the marinade over the chicken cubes and toss until thoroughly coated. Cover with plastic wrap and let marinate in the refrigerator for up to 8 hours.

2 Preheat the barbecue. Drain the chicken cubes, reserving the marinade. Thread the chicken onto several long metal skewers.

3 Cook the skewers over medium hot coals, turning and brushing frequently with the reserved marinade, for 6–10 minutes, or until thoroughly cooked. Transfer to a large serving plate, garnish with fresh chopped mint and citrus zest, and serve immediately.

italian deviled chicken

ingredients

SERVES 4

4 skinless, boneless chicken
    breasts, about 6 oz/175 g
    each, cut into 1-inch/
    2.5-cm cubes

1/2 cup olive oil

finely grated rind and juice
    of 1 lemon

2 garlic cloves, finely
    chopped

2 tsp finely chopped dried red
    chiles

salt and pepper

fresh flat-leaf parsley sprigs,
    to garnish

method

1 Place the chicken cubes in a large, shallow, nonmetallic dish. Place the olive oil, lemon rind and juice, garlic, and chiles in a measuring cup and stir until well blended. Season to taste with salt and pepper.

2 Pour the mixture over the chicken and stir gently to coat. Cover with plastic wrap and let marinate in the refrigerator for up to 8 hours.

3 Preheat the barbecue. Drain the chicken, reserving the marinade. Thread the chicken onto several presoaked wooden skewers and cook over medium hot coals, turning and brushing frequently with the reserved marinade, for 6–10 minutes, or until thoroughly cooked. Transfer to a large serving dish, garnish with parsley sprigs, and serve immediately.

turkey skewers with cilantro pesto

ingredients

SERVES 4

1 lb/450 g skinless, boneless
turkey, cut into 2-inch/
5-cm cubes

2 zucchini, thickly sliced

1 red and 1 yellow bell
pepper, seeded and cut
into 2-inch/5-cm squares

8 cherry tomatoes

8 pearl onions, peeled but left
whole

marinade

6 tbsp olive oil

3 tbsp dry white wine

1 tsp green peppercorns,
crushed

2 tbsp chopped fresh cilantro

salt

cilantro pesto

4 tbsp fresh cilantro leaves

1 tbsp fresh parsley leaves

1 garlic clove

$1/2$ cup pine nuts

$1/4$ cup freshly grated
Parmesan cheese

6 tbsp extra virgin olive oil

juice of 1 lemon

salt

method

1 Place the turkey in a large glass bowl. To make the marinade, mix the olive oil, wine, peppercorns, and cilantro together in a measuring cup and season to taste with salt. Pour the mixture over the turkey and turn until the turkey is thoroughly coated. Cover with plastic wrap and let marinate in the refrigerator for 2 hours.

2 Preheat the barbecue. To make the pesto, put the cilantro and parsley into a food processor and process until finely chopped. Add the Parmesan cheese, oil, lemon juice, and salt to taste, and process briefly to mix. Transfer to a bowl, cover, and let chill in the refrigerator until required.

3 Drain the turkey, reserving the marinade. Thread the turkey, zucchini slices, bell pepper pieces, cherry tomatoes, and onions alternately onto metal skewers. Cook over medium hot coals, turning and brushing frequently with the marinade, for 10 minutes. Serve immediately with the cilantro pesto.

spicy turkey & sausage kabobs

ingredients

MAKES 8

6 tbsp olive oil

2 garlic cloves, crushed

1 fresh red chile, seeded
    and chopped

12 oz/350 g turkey breast
    fillet

$10^{1}/_{2}$ oz/300 g chorizo sausage

1 apple

1 tbsp lemon juice

8 bay leaves

salt and pepper

method

1 Place the olive oil, garlic, chile, and salt and pepper to taste in a small screw-top jar and shake well to combine. Let stand for 1 hour for the garlic and chile to flavor the oil.

2 Preheat the barbecue. Using a sharp knife, cut the turkey into 1-inch/2.5-cm pieces. Cut the sausage into 1-inch/2.5-cm lengths. Cut the apple into chunks and remove the core. Toss the apple in the lemon juice to prevent discoloration.

3 Thread the turkey and sausage pieces onto 8 metal skewers, alternating with the apple chunks and bay leaves.

4 Cook the kabobs over hot coals for 15 minutes, or until the turkey is cooked through. Turn and baste the kabobs frequently with the flavored oil.

5 Transfer the kabobs to warmed serving plates and serve immediately.

caribbean fish kabobs

ingredients

SERVES 6

2 lb 4 oz/1 kg swordfish
   steaks

3 tbsp olive oil

3 tbsp lime juice

1 garlic clove, finely chopped

1 tsp paprika

3 onions, cut into wedges

6 tomatoes, cut into wedges

salt and pepper

method

1 Using a sharp knife, cut the fish into 1-inch/2.5-cm cubes and place in a shallow, nonmetallic dish. Place the oil, lime juice, garlic, and paprika in a measuring cup and mix. Season to taste with salt and pepper. Pour the marinade over the fish, turning to coat. Cover with plastic wrap and let marinate in the refrigerator for 1 hour.

2 Preheat the barbecue. Thread the fish cubes, onion, and tomato wedges alternately onto 6 long, presoaked wooden skewers. Set aside the marinade.

3 Cook the kabobs over medium hot coals for 8–10 minutes, turning and brushing frequently with the reserved marinade. When they are cooked through, transfer the kabobs to a large serving plate, and serve immediately.

coconut shrimp

ingredients

SERVES 4

6 scallions

1³/₄ cups coconut milk

finely grated rind and juice of
1 lime

4 tbsp chopped fresh cilantro,
plus extra to garnish

2 tbsp corn oil

1 lb 7 oz/650 g raw jumbo
shrimp, peeled and
deveined

pepper

lemon wedges, to garnish

method

1 Finely chop the scallions and place in a large, shallow, nonmetallic dish with the coconut milk, lime rind and juice, cilantro, and oil. Mix well and season to taste with pepper. Add the shrimp, turning to coat. Cover with plastic wrap and let marinate in the refrigerator for 1 hour.

2 Preheat the barbecue. Drain the shrimp, reserving the marinade. Thread the shrimp onto 8 long metal skewers.

3 Cook the skewers over medium hot coals, brushing with the reserved marinade and turning frequently, for 8 minutes, or until they have changed color. Serve the shrimp immediately, garnished with the lemon wedges and chopped cilantro.

charbroiled tuna & vegetable kabobs

ingredients

SERVES 4

4 tuna steaks, about
   5 oz/140 g each

2 red onions

12 cherry tomatoes

1 red bell pepper, seeded and
   diced into 1-inch/2.5-cm
   pieces

1 yellow bell pepper, seeded
   and diced into 1-inch/
   2.5-cm pieces

1 zucchini, sliced

1 tbsp chopped fresh oregano

4 tbsp olive oil

freshly ground black pepper

lime wedges, to garnish

salad greens, to serve

method

1 Preheat the barbecue. Cut the tuna into 1-inch/2.5-cm dice. Peel the onions, and cut each onion lengthwise into 6 wedges.

2 Divide the fish and vegetables evenly between 8 presoaked wooden skewers and arrange on an oiled rack.

3 Mix the oregano and oil together in a small bowl. Season to taste with pepper. Lightly brush the kabobs with the oil and cook over hot coals for 10–15 minutes, or until evenly cooked, turning occasionally.

4 Garnish with lime wedges and serve with salad greens.

monkfish & shrimp kabobs

ingredients

SERVES 4

1 lb 5 oz/600 g monkfish
1 green bell pepper
1 onion
3 tbsp olive oil
3 tbsp lemon juice
2 garlic cloves, crushed
16 large, fresh shrimp, peeled
  and deveined
16 fresh bay leaves
salt and pepper

method

1 Cut the monkfish into chunks measuring about 1 inch/2.5 cm. Cut the bell pepper into similar-size chunks, discarding the core and seeds. Cut the onion into 6 wedges, then cut each wedge in half widthwise and separate the layers.

2 To make the marinade, put the oil, lemon juice, garlic, and salt and pepper to taste in a bowl and whisk together. Add the monkfish, shrimp, onion, and bell pepper pieces and toss together until coated in the marinade. Cover and let marinate in the fridge for 2–3 hours.

3 Thread the pieces of fish, shrimp, bell pepper, onion, and bay leaves onto 8 greased, flat metal kabob skewers, alternating and dividing the ingredients as evenly as possible.

4 Preheat the barbecue. Cook the kabobs on an oiled rack over hot coals for 10–15 minutes, turning frequently and basting with any remaining marinade, until cooked and lightly charred. Serve hot, garnished with lemon wedges.

swordfish kabobs

ingredients

SERVES 4–6

1 lb 5 oz/600 g boneless
swordfish steaks, about
1 inch/2.5 cm thick and
cut into 1-inch/2.5-cm
cubes

20 fresh bay leaves

olive oil, for oiling

marinade

4 tbsp extra virgin olive oil

2 tbsp freshly squeezed
lemon juice

1 garlic clove, crushed to a
paste with $1/4$ tsp salt

$1/4$ tsp white pepper

pinch of hot or smoked
paprika, to taste

1 onion, halved and then cut
into semicircular shapes

4 fresh bay leaves, torn in half

dressing

5 tbsp extra virgin olive oil

5 tbsp freshly squeezed
lemon juice

2 tbsp chopped fresh dill

method

1 To make the marinade, whisk the oil, lemon juice, garlic, pepper, and paprika together in a nonreactive bowl. Add the swordfish cubes and use your hands to coat gently with the marinade. Sprinkle the onion and torn bay leaves over the top. Cover and let marinate in the refrigerator for at least 4 hours.

2 Meanwhile, make the dressing. Whisk all the ingredients together in a small bowl, cover, and set aside.

3 Put the whole bay leaves in a heatproof bowl, pour over enough boiling water to cover, and let soften for 1 hour. Drain well and pat dry.

4 Preheat the barbecue. Lightly brush 4 long, flat metal skewers with oil and thread an equal quantity of the swordfish cubes and 5 bay leaves onto each. Cook the kabobs on an oiled rack over hot coals for 10–15 minutes, turning frequently and basting with any remaining marinade, until the swordfish feels firm. Discard the bay leaves before eating and serve the swordfish with the dressing.

greek vegetable kabobs

ingredients

SERVES 4

2 onions

8 new potatoes, washed but not peeled

1 eggplant, cut into 8 pieces

8 thick slices cucumber

1 red bell pepper, seeded and cut into 8 pieces

1 yellow bell pepper, seeded and cut into 8 pieces

8 oz/225 g provolone cheese, cut into 8 cubes

2 nectarines, pitted and cut into wedges

8 button mushrooms

2 tbsp olive oil

2 tsp chopped fresh thyme

2 tsp chopped fresh rosemary

salt

Tzatziki, to serve

method

1 Preheat the barbecue. Cut the onions into wedges, then place the onions and potatoes in a pan of lightly salted boiling water and cook for 20 minutes, or until just tender. Drain and let cool. Meanwhile, blanch the eggplant in boiling water for 2 minutes, then add the cucumber and let simmer for 1 minute. Add the bell peppers and let simmer for 2 minutes, then drain and let the vegetables cool.

2 Place the cooled vegetables, cheese, nectarines, and mushrooms in a bowl. Add the olive oil and herbs and toss to coat. Thread the vegetables, cheese, nectarines, and mushrooms onto several metal skewers.

3 Cook the kabobs over hot coals, turning frequently, for 15 minutes. Transfer to a large serving plate and serve immediately with the Tzatziki.

vegetable brochettes

ingredients

SERVES 4

2 zucchini

1 yellow bell pepper, seeded
    and quartered

8 oz/225 g firm tofu (drained
    weight)

4 cherry tomatoes

4 pearl onions

8 white mushrooms

honey glaze

2 tbsp olive oil

1 tbsp mustard

1 tbsp honey

salt and pepper

method

1 Preheat the barbecue. Using a vegetable peeler, peel off strips of skin along the length of the zucchini to create alternate yellow-and-green stripes, then cut each zucchini into 8 thick slices. Cut each of the yellow bell pepper quarters in half. Cut the drained tofu into 1-inch/2.5-cm cubes.

2 Thread the pieces of bell pepper, zucchini slices, tofu cubes, cherry tomatoes, pearl onions, and white mushrooms onto 4 metal skewers.

3 To make the glaze, mix the olive oil, mustard, and honey together in a measuring cup and season to taste with salt and pepper.

4 Brush the brochettes with the honey glaze and cook over medium hot coals, turning and brushing frequently with the glaze, for 8–10 minutes. Serve.

marinated tofu skewers

ingredients

SERVES 4

12 oz/350 g firm tofu
1 red bell pepper
1 yellow bell pepper
2 zucchini
8 button mushrooms

marinade

grated rind and juice of
$1/2$ lemon
1 garlic clove, crushed
$1/2$ tsp chopped fresh
rosemary
$1/2$ tsp chopped fresh thyme
1 tbsp walnut oil

to garnish

shredded carrot
lemon wedges

method

1 To make the marinade, mix the lemon rind and juice, garlic, rosemary, thyme, and walnut oil together in a shallow dish. Drain the tofu, pat it dry on paper towels, and cut it into squares. Add to the marinade and toss to coat. Let marinate for 20–30 minutes.

2 Preheat the barbecue. Seed the bell peppers and cut into 1-inch/2.5-cm pieces. Blanch in boiling water for 4 minutes, refresh in cold water, and drain. Using a channel knife or potato peeler, remove strips of peel from the zucchini. Cut the zucchini into 1-inch/2.5-cm chunks.

3 Remove the tofu from the marinade, reserving the liquid for basting. Thread the tofu onto 8 presoaked wooden skewers, alternating with the bell peppers, zucchini, and mushrooms.

4 Cook the skewers over medium hot coals for 6 minutes, turning and basting with the marinade. Transfer the skewers to warmed serving plates, garnish with shredded carrot and lemon wedges, and serve.

spicy caribbean kabobs

ingredients

SERVES 4

1 ear of corn

1 chayote, peeled and
   cut into chunks

1 ripe plantain, peeled and
   cut into thick slices

1 eggplant, cut into chunks

1 red bell pepper, seeded and
   cut into chunks

1 green bell pepper, seeded
   and cut into chunks

1 onion, cut into wedges

8 white mushrooms

4 cherry tomatoes

marinade

2/3 cup tomato juice

4 tbsp corn oil

4 tbsp lime juice

3 tbsp dark soy sauce

1 shallot, finely chopped

2 garlic cloves, finely
   chopped

1 fresh green chile, seeded
   and finely chopped

1/2 tsp ground cinnamon

pepper

method

1 Using a sharp knife, remove the husks and silks from the corn and cut into 1-inch/2.5-cm thick slices. Blanch the chayote chunks in boiling water for 2 minutes. Drain, refresh under cold running water, and drain again. Place the chayote chunks in a large bowl with the corn slices and the remaining ingredients.

2 Mix all the marinade ingredients together in a measuring cup, seasoning to taste with pepper. Pour the marinade over the vegetables, tossing to coat. Cover with plastic wrap and let marinate in the refrigerator for 3 hours.

3 Preheat the barbecue. Drain the vegetables, reserving the marinade. Thread the vegetables onto several metal skewers. Cook over hot coals, turning and brushing frequently with the reserved marinade, for 10–15 minutes. Transfer to a large serving plate and serve immediately.

cheese & red onion kabobs

ingredients

SERVES 4

3 red onions

1 lb/450 g provolone cheese,
cut into 1-inch/2.5-cm
cubes

2 tart apples, cored and cut
into wedges

4 tbsp olive oil

1 tbsp cider vinegar

1 tbsp Dijon mustard

1 garlic clove, finely chopped

1 tsp finely chopped sage

salt and pepper

method

1 Cut the onions into wedges, then place in a large, shallow, nonmetallic dish with the cheese and apples. Mix the oil, vinegar, mustard, garlic, and sage together in a measuring cup and season to taste with salt and pepper.

2 Pour the marinade over the onions, cheese, and apples, tossing to coat. Cover with plastic wrap and let marinate in the refrigerator for 2 hours.

3 Preheat the barbecue. Drain the onions, cheese, and apples, reserving the marinade. Thread the onions, cheese, and apples alternately onto several metal skewers. Cook over hot coals, turning and brushing frequently with the reserved marinade, for 10–15 minutes. Transfer to a large serving plate and serve immediately.

on the side

While most attention is focused on what happens center stage on the grill, for a really successful barbecue, it is important to give some thought to side dishes, sauces, and relishes. Salads are an easy option because they can be prepared in advance and, if you include one made with potatoes, pasta, rice, or other grains, you won't have to worry about cooking any accompaniments on the day.

If there is room on the barbecue grill, it is fun to include vegetable packages, chargrilled corn cobs, or crisp potato skins. Ever popular, garlic bread is a convenient compromise because, once prepared, all it requires is gentle warming on the side of the grill.

Homemade dressings and sauces are more flavorsome, economical, and often healthier than prepared types. It's good to offer a choice but to save yourself too much work, bear in mind that some will double up. Hummus, for example, is lovely with summer vegetables and also a perfect accompaniment to lamb, guacamole is the ideal partner for steak, kabobs, and chargrilled vegetables, while a spicy barbecue sauce is equally good with sausages, burgers, and chops.

Try to make sure that side dishes, especially any made with mayonnaise, such as coleslaw are placed in the shade. Don't forget a supply of serving spoons.

corn on the cob

ingredients

SERVES 4

4 corn cobs, with husks

7 tbsp butter

1 tbsp chopped fresh parsley

1 tsp chopped fresh chives

1 tsp chopped fresh thyme

grated rind of 1 lemon

salt and pepper

method

1 Preheat the barbecue. To prepare the corn cobs, peel back the husks and remove the silk. Fold the husks back around the kernels and secure them in place with string if necessary.

2 Blanch the corn cobs in a large pan of boiling water for 5 minutes. Remove with a slotted spoon and drain thoroughly. Cook the corn cobs over medium hot coals for 20–30 minutes, turning frequently.

3 Meanwhile, soften the butter and beat in the parsley, chives, thyme, lemon rind, and salt and pepper to taste. Transfer the corn cobs to serving plates, remove the string, and pull back the husks. Serve each with a generous portion of herb butter.

zucchini & cheese packages

ingredients

SERVES 2

1 small bunch of fresh mint

2 large zucchini

1 tbsp olive oil, plus extra
    for brushing

4 oz/115 g feta cheese,
    cut into strips

pepper

method

1 Preheat the barbecue. Using a sharp knife, finely chop enough mint to fill 1 tablespoon. Set aside until required. Cut out 2 rectangles of foil, each large enough to enclose a zucchini, and brush lightly with olive oil. Cut a few slits along the length of each zucchini and place them on the foil rectangles.

2 Insert strips of feta cheese along the slits in the zucchini, then drizzle the olive oil over the top, sprinkle with the reserved chopped mint, and season to taste with pepper. Fold in the sides of the foil rectangles securely and seal the edges to enclose the cheese-filled zucchini completely.

3 Bake the packages in the barbecue embers for 30–40 minutes. Carefully unwrap the packages and serve immediately.

stuffed mushrooms

ingredients

SERVES 12

12 portobello mushrooms

4 tsp olive oil

4 scallions, chopped

2 cups fresh brown
  breadcrumbs

1 tsp chopped fresh oregano

$3^1/2$ oz/100 g feta cheese
  or chorizo sausage

corn oil, for oiling

method

1 Preheat the barbecue. Remove the stems from the mushrooms and chop the stems finely. Heat half of the olive oil in a large skillet. Add the mushroom stems and scallions and cook briefly.

2 Mix the mushroom stems and scallions together in a large bowl.

3 Add the breadcrumbs and oregano to the mushrooms and scallions, mix well, then reserve until required.

4 If you are using feta, crumble the cheese into small pieces in a small bowl. If you are using chorizo sausage, remove the skin and chop the flesh finely.

5 Add the crumbled feta cheese or chopped chorizo to the breadcrumb mixture and mix well. Spoon the stuffing mixture into the mushroom caps.

6 Drizzle the remaining olive oil over the stuffed mushrooms, then cook on an oiled rack over medium hot coals for 8–10 minutes. Transfer the mushrooms to individual serving plates and serve while still hot.

stuffed tomato packages

ingredients

SERVES 4

1 tbsp olive oil

2 tbsp sunflower seeds

1 onion, finely chopped

1 garlic clove, finely chopped

1 lb 2 oz/500 g fresh spinach,
thick stalks removed and
leaves shredded

pinch of freshly grated
nutmeg

4 beefsteak tomatoes

5 oz/140 g mozzarella
cheese, diced

salt and pepper

method

1 Preheat the barbecue. Heat the oil in a heavy-bottom pan. Add the sunflower seeds and cook, stirring constantly, for 2 minutes, or until golden. Add the onion and cook over low heat, stirring occasionally, for 5 minutes, or until softened but not browned. Add the garlic and spinach, cover, and cook for 2–3 minutes, or until the spinach has wilted. Remove the pan from the heat and season to taste with nutmeg, salt, and pepper. Let cool.

2 Using a sharp knife, cut off and set aside a thin slice from the top of each tomato and scoop out the flesh with a teaspoon, being careful not to pierce the shell. Chop the flesh and stir it into the spinach mixture with the mozzarella cheese.

3 Fill the tomato shells with the spinach and cheese mixture and replace the tops. Cut 4 squares of foil, each large enough to enclose a tomato. Place one tomato in the center of each square and fold up the sides to enclose securely. Cook over hot coals, turning occasionally, for 10 minutes. Serve immediately in the foil packages.

potato fans

ingredients

SERVES 6

6 large potatoes, scrubbed
   but not peeled
1 garlic clove, finely chopped
2 tbsp olive oil
salt and pepper

method

1 Preheat the barbecue. Using a sharp knife, make a series of cuts across the potatoes almost all the way through. Cut out 6 squares of foil, each large enough to enclose a potato, and place a potato on top of each one.

2 Mix together the garlic and olive oil and brush generously over the potatoes. Season with salt and pepper to taste. Fold up the sides of the foil to enclose the potatoes completely.

3 Cook over hot coals, turning occasionally, for 1 hour. To serve, open the foil packages and gently pinch the potatoes to open up the fans.

crispy potato skins

ingredients

SERVES 4–6

8 small baking potatoes, scrubbed
3½ tbsp butter, melted
salt and pepper

topping

6 scallions, sliced
½ cup grated Gruyère cheese
1¾ oz/50 g salami, cut into thin strips

method

1 Preheat the oven to 400°F/200°C. Prick the potato skins with a fork and bake in the oven for 1 hour, or until tender. Alternatively, cook in a microwave on High for 12–15 minutes. Cut the potatoes in half and scoop out the flesh, leaving about ¼ inch/5 mm potato flesh lining the skin.

2 Preheat the barbecue. Brush the insides of the potato skins with melted butter.

3 Place the skins, cut-side down, over medium hot coals and cook for 10–15 minutes. Turn the potato skins over and cook for an additional 5 minutes, or until they are crispy. Be careful that they do not burn. Season the potato skins with salt and pepper to taste and serve while they are still warm.

4 If desired, the skins can be filled with a variety of toppings. Grill the potato skins as above for 10 minutes, then turn cut-side up and sprinkle with slices of scallion, grated cheese, and chopped salami. Cook for an additional 5 minutes, or until the cheese begins to melt. Serve hot.

potato salad

ingredients

SERVES 4

1 lb 9 oz/700 g tiny new
    potatoes
8 scallions
1 hard-cooked egg (optional)
1 cup mayonnaise
1 tsp paprika
salt and pepper

to garnish
2 tbsp snipped fresh chives
pinch of paprika

method

1 Bring a large pan of lightly salted water to a boil. Add the potatoes and cook for 10–15 minutes, or until just tender.

2 Drain the potatoes and rinse them under cold running water until completely cold. Drain again. Transfer the potatoes to a bowl and reserve until required. Using a sharp knife, slice the scallions thinly on the diagonal. Chop the hard-cooked egg, if using.

3 Mix the mayonnaise, paprika, and salt and pepper to taste together in a bowl. Pour the mixture over the potatoes. Add the scallions and egg, if using, to the potatoes and toss together.

4 Transfer the potato salad to a serving bowl and sprinkle with snipped chives and a pinch of paprika. Cover and let chill in the refrigerator until required.

garlic bread

ingredients

SERVES 6

2/3 cup butter, softened
3 garlic cloves, crushed
2 tbsp chopped fresh parsley
pepper
1 large or 2 small loaves of
    French bread

method

1 Mix together the butter, garlic, and parsley in a bowl until well combined. Season with pepper to taste and mix well.

2 Cut a few lengthwise slits in the French bread. Spread the flavored butter inside the slits and place the bread on a large sheet of thick aluminum foil.

3 Preheat the barbecue. Wrap the bread well in the foil and cook over hot coals for 10–15 minutes, until the butter melts and the bread is piping hot.

4 Serve as an accompaniment to a wide range of dishes.

panzanella

ingredients

SERVES 4–6

9 oz/250 g stale focaccia,
     ciabatta, or French bread
4 large, vine-ripened
     tomatoes
about 6 tbsp extra virgin
     olive oil
4 red, yellow, and/or orange
     bell peppers
3 1/2 oz/100 g cucumber
1 large red onion, finely
     chopped
8 canned anchovy fillets,
     drained and chopped
2 tbsp capers in brine, rinsed
     and patted dry
about 4 tbsp red wine vinegar
about 2 tbsp best-quality
     balsamic vinegar
salt and pepper
fresh basil leaves, to garnish

method

1 Cut the bread into 1-inch/2.5-cm cubes and place in a large bowl. Working over a plate to catch any juices, quarter the tomatoes; reserve the juices. Using a teaspoon, scoop out the cores and seeds and discard, then finely chop the flesh. Add to the bread cubes.

2 Drizzle 5 tablespoons of the olive oil over the mixture and toss with your hands until well coated. Pour in the reserved tomato juice and toss again. Set aside for about 30 minutes.

3 Meanwhile, cut the bell peppers in half and remove the cores and seeds. Place on a metal rack under a preheated hot broiler and broil for 10 minutes, or until the skins are charred and the flesh softened. Place in a plastic bag, seal, and set aside for 20 minutes to allow the steam to loosen the skins. Remove the skins, then finely chop.

4 Cut the cucumber in half lengthwise, then cut each half into 3 strips lengthwise. Using a teaspoon, scoop out and discard the seeds. Dice the cucumber.

5 Add the onion, peppers, cucumber, anchovy fillets, and capers to the bread and toss together. Sprinkle with the red wine and balsamic vinegars and season to taste with salt and pepper. Drizzle with extra olive oil or vinegar if necessary, but be cautious so that it does not become too greasy or soggy. Sprinkle the fresh basil leaves over the salad and serve at once.

chargrilled vegetables with creamy pesto

ingredients

SERVES 4

1 red onion

1 fennel bulb

4 baby eggplants

4 baby zucchini

1 orange bell pepper

1 red bell pepper

2 beefsteak tomatoes

2 tbsp olive oil

salt and pepper

1 fresh basil sprig, to garnish

creamy pesto

4 tbsp fresh basil leaves

1 tbsp pine nuts

1 garlic clove

pinch of coarse sea salt

$1/4$ cup freshly grated
    Parmesan cheese

$1/4$ cup extra virgin olive oil

$2/3$ cup strained plain yogurt

method

1 Preheat the barbecue. To make the creamy pesto, place the basil, pine nuts, garlic, and sea salt in a mortar and pound to a paste with a pestle. Gradually work in the Parmesan cheese, then gradually stir in the oil.

2 Place the yogurt in a small serving bowl and stir in 3–4 tablespoons of the pesto mixture. Cover with plastic wrap and let chill in the refrigerator until required. Store any leftover pesto mixture in a screw-top jar in the refrigerator.

3 Prepare the vegetables. Cut the onion and fennel bulb into wedges, trim and slice the eggplants and zucchini, seed and thickly slice the bell peppers, and cut the tomatoes in half. Brush the vegetables with oil and season to taste with salt and pepper.

4 Cook the eggplants and bell peppers over hot coals for 3 minutes, then add the zucchini, onion, fennel, and tomatoes and cook, turning occasionally and brushing with more oil if necessary, for an additional 5 minutes. Transfer to a large serving plate and serve with the pesto, garnished with a basil sprig.

summer vegetable packages

ingredients

SERVES 4

2 lb 4 oz/1 kg mixed baby
vegetables, such as
carrots, asparagus, baby
corn, cherry tomatoes,
leeks, zucchini, chiles,
and onions

1 lemon

1/2 cup unsalted butter

3 tbsp chopped mixed fresh
herbs, such as parsley,
thyme, chives, and chervil

2 garlic cloves

salt and pepper

method

1 Preheat the barbecue. Cut out 4 x 12-inch/
30-cm squares of foil and divide the
vegetables equally among them.

2 Using a grater, finely grate the lemon rind,
then squeeze the juice from the lemon and set
aside until required. Put the lemon rind,
butter, herbs, and garlic into a food processor
and process until blended, then season to
taste with salt and pepper. Alternatively, beat
together in a bowl until blended.

3 Divide the butter equally among the
vegetables, dotting it on top. Fold up the sides
of the foil to enclose the vegetables, sealing
securely. Cook over medium hot coals, turning
occasionally, for 25–30 minutes. Open the
packages, sprinkle with the reserved lemon
juice, and serve immediately.

pasta salad with basil vinaigrette

ingredients

SERVES 4

8 oz/225 g dried fusilli

4 tomatoes

scant 1/3 cup black olives

1 oz/25 g sun-dried tomatoes
   in oil

2 tbsp pine nuts

2 tbsp freshly grated
   Parmesan cheese

salt and pepper

fresh basil leaves, to garnish

vinaigrette

1/2 oz/15 g basil leaves

1 garlic clove, crushed

2 tbsp freshly grated
   Parmesan cheese

4 tbsp extra virgin olive oil

2 tbsp lemon juice

method

1 Cook the pasta in a large pan of lightly salted boiling water for 10–12 minutes, or until just tender but still firm to the bite. Drain the pasta, rinse under cold running water, then drain again thoroughly. Place the pasta in a large bowl.

2 Preheat the broiler to medium. To make the vinaigrette, place the basil leaves, garlic, cheese, olive oil, and lemon juice in a food processor. Season to taste with salt and pepper and process until the leaves are well chopped and the ingredients are combined. Alternatively, finely chop the basil leaves by hand and combine with the other vinaigrette ingredients. Pour the vinaigrette over the pasta and toss to coat.

3 Cut the tomatoes into wedges. Pit and halve the olives. Slice the sun-dried tomatoes. Toast the pine nuts on a cookie sheet under the hot broiler until golden.

4 Add the tomatoes (fresh and sun-dried) and the olives to the pasta and mix until combined.

5 Transfer the pasta mixture to a serving dish, sprinkle over the Parmesan and toasted pine nuts, and serve garnished with a few basil leaves.

tropical rice salad

ingredients

$^{1}/_{2}$ cup long-grain rice

4 scallions

8 oz/225 g canned pineapple
   chunks in natural juice

7 oz/200 g canned corn,
   drained

2 red bell peppers, seeded
   and diced

3 tbsp golden raisins

salt and pepper

dressing

1 tbsp peanut oil

1 tbsp hazelnut oil

1 tbsp light soy sauce

1 garlic clove, finely chopped

1 tsp chopped fresh ginger

method

1 Cook the rice in a large pan of lightly salted boiling water for 15 minutes, or until tender. Drain thoroughly and rinse under cold running water. Place the rice in a large serving bowl.

2 Using a sharp knife, finely chop the scallions. Drain the pineapple chunks, reserving the juice in a measuring cup. Add the pineapple chunks, corn, red bell peppers, chopped scallions, and golden raisins to the rice and mix lightly.

3 Add all the dressing ingredients to the reserved pineapple juice, whisking well, and season to taste with salt and pepper. Pour the dressing over the salad and toss until the salad is thoroughly coated. Serve immediately.

green bean & feta salad

ingredients

SERVES 4

12 oz/350 g green beans, trimmed

1 red onion, chopped

$^3/_4$ tbsp chopped fresh cilantro

2 radishes, thinly sliced

$^3/_4$ cup crumbled feta cheese

1 tsp chopped fresh oregano or $^1/_2$ tsp dried oregano

2 tbsp red wine or fruit vinegar

5 tbsp extra virgin olive oil

6 ripe cherry or small tomatoes, quartered

pepper

method

1 Bring about 2 inches/5 cm of water to a boil in the bottom of a steamer or in a medium saucepan. Add the green beans to the top of the steamer or place them in a metal colander set over the pan of water. Cover and steam for about 5 minutes, until just tender.

2 Transfer the beans to a bowl and add the onion, cilantro, radishes, and crumbled feta cheese.

3 Sprinkle the oregano over the salad, then grind pepper over to taste. Whisk the vinegar and olive oil together and then pour over the salad. Toss gently to mix well.

4 Transfer to a serving platter, surround with the tomato quarters, and serve at once or chill until ready to serve.

tabbouleh

ingredients

SERVES 4

1 cup bulgur wheat

3 tbsp extra virgin olive oil

4 tbsp lemon juice

4 scallions

1 green bell pepper, seeded
   and sliced

4 tomatoes, chopped

2 tbsp chopped fresh parsley

2 tbsp chopped fresh mint

8 black olives, pitted

salt and pepper

fresh mint sprigs, to garnish

method

1 Place the bulgur wheat in a large bowl and add enough cold water to cover. Let stand for 30 minutes, or until the wheat has doubled in size. Drain well and press out as much liquid as possible. Spread out the wheat on paper towels to dry.

2 Place the wheat in a serving bowl. Mix the olive oil and lemon juice together in a measuring cup and season to taste with salt and pepper. Pour the lemon mixture over the wheat and let marinate for 1 hour.

3 Using a sharp knife, finely chop the scallions, then add to the salad with the green bell pepper, tomatoes, parsley, and mint, and toss lightly to mix. Top the salad with the olives and garnish with fresh mint sprigs, then serve.

homemade tomato sauce

ingredients

SERVES 2–4

1 tbsp butter

2 tbsp olive oil

1 onion, chopped

1 garlic clove, finely chopped

14 oz/400 g canned tomatoes
   or 1 lb/450 g fresh
   tomatoes, peeled

1 tbsp tomato paste

generous $1/2$ cup red wine

$2/3$ cup vegetable stock

$1/2$ tsp sugar

1 bay leaf

salt and pepper

method

1 Melt the butter with the oil in a large pan over medium heat, add the onion and garlic, and cook, stirring frequently, for 5 minutes, or until the onion has softened and is beginning to brown.

2 Add all the remaining ingredients to the pan and season to taste with salt and pepper. Bring to a boil, then reduce the heat to low and let simmer, uncovered and stirring occasionally, for 30 minutes, or until the tomato sauce has thickened.

3 Remove and discard the bay leaf, pour the sauce into a food processor or blender, and process until smooth. Alternatively, using the back of a wooden spoon, push the sauce through a nylon strainer into a bowl.

4 If serving at once, reheat the sauce gently in a pan. Alternatively, store and reheat before serving.

spicy barbecue sauce

ingredients

SERVES 4

2 tbsp corn oil

1 large onion, chopped

2 garlic cloves, chopped

1 cup canned chopped
    tomatoes

1 tbsp Worcestershire sauce

2 tbsp fruity brown sauce

2 tbsp brown sugar

4 tbsp white wine vinegar

$1/2$ tsp mild chili powder

$1/4$ tsp dry mustard

dash of Tabasco sauce

salt and pepper

cooked sausages or burgers
    in bread rolls, to serve

method

1 To make the sauce, heat the oil in a small pan and cook the onion and garlic for 4–5 minutes, or until softened and just beginning to brown.

2 Add the tomatoes, Worcestershire sauce, brown sauce, sugar, vinegar, chili powder, dry mustard, and Tabasco sauce to the pan. Add salt and pepper to taste, and bring to a boil.

3 Reduce the heat and simmer gently for 10–15 minutes, or until the sauce begins to thicken slightly. Stir occasionally so that the sauce does not burn and stick to the bottom of the pan. Set aside and keep warm until required. Serve with sausages or burgers.

coleslaw

ingredients

SERVES 10–12

²/₃ cup mayonnaise

²/₃ cup low-fat plain yogurt

dash of Tabasco sauce

1 medium head of white
   cabbage

4 carrots

1 green bell pepper

salt and pepper

method

1 To make the dressing, mix the mayonnaise, yogurt, Tabasco sauce, and salt and pepper to taste together in a small bowl. Chill in the refrigerator until required.

2 Cut the cabbage in half and then into quarters. Remove and discard the tough center stem. Shred the cabbage leaves finely. Wash the leaves under cold running water and dry thoroughly on paper towels. Peel the carrots and shred in a food processor or on a mandoline. Alternatively, roughly grate the carrot. Cut the bell pepper into quarters, then seed it and cut the flesh into thin strips.

3 Put the vegetables together in a large serving bowl and toss to mix. Pour over the dressing and toss until the vegetables are well coated. Let the vegetable mixture chill until required.

mayonnaise

ingredients

2 large egg yolks

2 tsp Dijon mustard

$^3/_4$ tsp salt, or to taste

white pepper

2 tbsp lemon juice or white wine vinegar

about $1^1/_4$ cups sunflower oil

method

1 Blend the egg yolks with the Dijon mustard, salt, and white pepper to taste in a food processor or blender or by hand. Add the lemon juice and blend again.

2 With the motor still running or still beating, add the oil, drop by drop at first. When the sauce begins to thicken, add the oil in a slow, steady stream. Taste and adjust the seasoning with extra salt, pepper, and lemon juice, if necessary. If the sauce seems too thick, slowly add 1 tablespoon hot water, light cream, or lemon juice.

3 Use at once or store in an airtight container in the refrigerator for up to 1 week.

tzatziki

ingredients

SERVES 4

1 small cucumber

1¼ cups strained plain yogurt

1 large garlic clove, crushed

1 tbsp chopped fresh mint
    or dill

salt and pepper

warm pita bread, to serve

method

1 Peel, then coarsely grate the cucumber. Put in a strainer and squeeze out as much of the water as possible. Put the cucumber into a bowl.

2 Add the yogurt, garlic, and chopped mint (reserve a little as a garnish, if desired) to the cucumber and season with pepper. Mix well together and chill in the refrigerator for about 2 hours before serving.

3 To serve, stir the cucumber and yogurt dip and transfer to a serving bowl. Sprinkle with salt and accompany with warmed pita bread.

aïoli

ingredients

SERVES 2–4

3 large garlic cloves, finely
  chopped
2 egg yolks
1 cup extra virgin olive oil
1 tbsp lemon juice
1 tbsp lime juice
1 tbsp Dijon mustard
1 tbsp chopped fresh
  tarragon
salt and pepper
1 fresh tarragon sprig,
  to garnish

method

1 Make sure all the ingredients are at room temperature. Place the garlic and egg yolks in a food processor and process until well blended. With the motor running, pour in the oil, teaspoon by teaspoon, through the feeder tube until the mixture starts to thicken, then pour in the remaining oil in a thin stream until a thick mayonnaise forms.

2 Add the lemon and lime juices, mustard, and tarragon and season to taste with salt and pepper. Blend until smooth, then transfer to a nonmetallic bowl. Garnish with a tarragon sprig. Cover with plastic wrap and let chill until required.

hummus

ingredients

SERVES 8

8 oz/225 g dried chickpeas,
   covered with water and
   soaked overnight
juice of 2 large lemons
$^2/_3$ cup tahini paste
2 garlic cloves, crushed
4 tbsp extra-virgin olive oil
small pinch of ground cumin
salt and pepper
warm pita bread, to serve

to garnish

1 tsp paprika
chopped flat-leaf parsley

method

1 Drain the chickpeas, put in a saucepan, and cover with cold water. Bring to a boil, then simmer for about 2 hours, until very tender.

2 Drain the chickpeas, reserving a little of the liquid, and put in a food processor, reserving a few to garnish. Blend the chickpeas until smooth, gradually adding the lemon juice and enough reserved liquid to form a smooth, thick puree. Add the tahini paste, garlic, 3 tablespoons of the olive oil, and the cumin and blend until smooth. Season with salt and pepper.

3 Turn the mixture into a shallow serving dish and chill in the refrigerator for 2–3 hours before serving. To serve, mix the reserved olive oil with the paprika and drizzle over the top of the dish. Sprinkle with the parsley and the reserved chickpeas. Accompany with warm pita bread.

guacamole

ingredients

SERVES 4

2 large, ripe avocados

juice of 1 lime, or to taste

2 tsp olive oil

$1/2$ onion, finely chopped

1 fresh green chile, such as
poblano, seeded and
finely chopped

1 garlic clove, crushed

$1/4$ tsp ground cumin

1 tbsp chopped fresh cilantro

salt and pepper

tortilla chips, to serve

fresh dill or cilantro sprigs,
to garnish

method

1 Cut the avocados in half lengthwise and twist the 2 halves in opposite directions to separate. Carefully stab the pit with the point of a sharp knife and lift out.

2 Peel, then coarsely chop the avocado halves and place in a nonmetallic bowl. Squeeze over the lime juice and add the oil. Mash the avocados with a fork until the desired consistency is achieved—either chunky or smooth. Blend in the onion, chile, garlic, cumin, and chopped cilantro, then season to taste with salt and pepper.

3 Transfer to a serving dish and serve at once, to avoid discoloration, with tortilla chips and garnished with fresh dill sprigs.

tomato salsa

ingredients

SERVES 6

1 lb/450 g firm, ripe tomatoes

1 fresh jalapeño or other
    small hot chile

2 tsp extra virgin olive oil

1 garlic clove, crushed

grated rind and juice of 1 lime

pinch of sugar

4 tbsp chopped cilantro

salt

cilantro sprigs, to garnish

method

1 Using a sharp knife, finely dice the tomatoes and put into a bowl with the seeds. Halve the chile, remove and discard the seeds, and very finely dice the flesh. Add to the tomatoes.

2 Add all the remaining ingredients to the tomatoes, season to taste with salt, and mix well together.

3 Turn the mixture into a small, nonmetallic serving bowl, cover, and let stand at room temperature for 30 minutes to let the flavors combine. If not being served right away, the salsa can be stored in the refrigerator for up to 2–3 days, but it is best if allowed to return to room temperature for 1 hour before being served. Serve garnished with cilantro sprigs.